Advent

A spiritual focus for personal or group use

Joy

D1514045

A 31-DAY GUIDE

ELIZABETH RUNDLE

Copyright © 2005 CWR

Published 2005 by CWR, Waverley Abbey House, Waverley Lane, Farnham, Surrey GU9 8EP, England.

The right of Elizabeth Rundle to be identified as the author of this work has been asserted by her in accordance with the Copyright, Designs and Patents Act 1988, sections 77 and 78.

See back of book for list of National Distributors.

Unless otherwise indicated, all Scripture references are from the Holy Bible: New International Version (NIV), copyright © 1973, 1978, 1984 by the International Bible Society.

Front cover image: Stock Exchange

Concept development, editing, design and production by CWR

Printed in Malta by Gutenberg Press

ISBN 1-85345-356-0

Contents

Introduction

Exploring the impact of biblical 'joy' ...

Holiday companies fiercely compete to entice customers
to leave behind the gloom of winter and find renewing
sunshine. These short breaks, we're assured, are bound to
do us good and, once having taken their special offer, we
will all feel younger and happier!

So how about taking this idea into our spiritual lives?

Sometimes we really need a break from the commercial
momentum of singing cash tills and the glad tidings that
there are only x days before Christmas Day. Where on
earth have those 11 months gone since we vowed we
would *not* leave things to the last minute *next* year! Yes,
perhaps a short 15-minute break each day with an Advent
theme would give our hearts a lift and renew our spiritual
lives in a deeper knowledge and love of God's Son, Jesus
Christ.

By joy, I do not mean an effervescent froth of contrived
jollity. We are looking at a genuine, heartfelt radiance,
the joy that comes from a personal relationship with
Jesus Christ. I recall meeting this radiance on the face of
Jackie Pullinger as she led a Bible study for young men
in Hong Kong. In a dingy, sweaty, upstairs room, the lads
who had experienced drugs and crime were beaming
with enjoyment as they argued and learned about Jesus.
Jackie's face shone with unconditional love for these lads.

Joy holds a rich meaning and prompts a spontaneous
ripple effect.

For many people, preparation for Lent has become an
annual routine, but Advent still remains more difficult
to plan as a devotional area of growth. The first Advent
book I ever read was *Feast for Advent* by Delia Smith.
I was conscious that even though the story was so
familiar, I needed time to reflect on the themes and the
people involved with Jesus, Son of Mary, Messiah. For
me, Advent took on a new meaning and the words and

carols read at services became far more precious. God's amazing, breathtaking plan for salvation can actually be charted, and we read how Jesus the baby entered into the religious and political atmosphere of first-century Palestine.

The birth of Jesus into the world 2,000 years ago and the mystery and miracle today of His coming to each waiting heart is God's priceless gift, a gift we cannot receive with just a cursory 'thanks' on 25 December. It is a life-changing gift which enables us to enter into the preparations for both secular and spiritual Christmas with warm joy and gratitude.

A Christmas without Christ is meaningless – His life was prophesied, His teaching revolutionised legalistic ritual into a joyous, loving response to almighty God. His death and resurrection motivated His followers into a new way of living in peace, justice and love.

I hope you will be able to find fresh relevance and new insight in these next few weeks which will enrich your Christmas and permeate your whole life.

I wish you Advent joy.

Suggestions for Using *Advent Joy*

These devotions through the 31 days of December are designed for personal use or to share within the support and encouragement of a group.

If you are using the guide on your own, then each day will take about 15 minutes. The section for discussion could be glanced at and a couple of questions picked out to think about during the day. You will need a Bible and perhaps a small pad or diary. You might find it helpful to jot down a few comments or personal prayer needs each day.

For use with a group

For group use, it would be best if each member were to commit also to the daily devotions. The group material combines strands from the daily sessions as well as branching into ordinary life routine. The last three days offer a launch pad for further group meetings as the new year dawns.

Material for use with two or more people is found at the end of each week. The resources vary and are optional, as some may find they would like to discuss items from the daily section.

Elizabeth Rundle
2005

The Kingdom of God is Justice and Peace

1 DEC

A light has dawned ...

Switching on the Christmas lights has become a special feature in many villages, towns and cities. It seems we not only like our high streets to twinkle goodwill but houses and gardens now compete to spread festive joy. Lights attract – light is a vital element for life. God's first 'word' was 'Let there be light' and, thereafter, biblical imagery equated light with goodness and darkness with evil. Have you ever paused to think how tiny a light bulb is in comparison with the area it lights up? Our Advent challenge is to light up the areas where we live and work with Christ's joy and love; a lasting joy and love that is not put away with the Christmas decorations!

Bible reading
Isaiah 9:1–2, 6–7

Context
The book of Isaiah stands out in the Old Testament as the greatest book of prophecy. The God-inspired vision we are looking at today, is one of the best-known and best-loved of all prophecies and there will hardly be a service of nine readings and carols where this passage is not used. Uttered some seven centuries before the birth of Jesus, against the background of Assyrian invasion and oppression, verses 2 to 7 most probably became associated with the coronation of King Hezekiah. It was a 'hymn' heralding a new beginning – the people could draw a line under the past – no more the gloom of

domination but a glorious Messianic hope. Notice how this hope is rooted in the dynasty of David, the iconic shepherd king of their nation's golden era. Imagine Jesus learning this prophecy in the Nazareth synagogue!

Reflection

Perhaps some of our earliest words have been encouraged by nursery rhymes and it's amazing how far into old age and even dementia, hymns and poetry still touch the soul. These long-ago prophecies were methodically learned and recited and became a living hope for God's people. The son born of King David's lineage would embody God Himself and bring to the world a completely new way of life.

God gave Isaiah the vision of a newborn baby, the perfect symbol for hope and joy. Have you noticed how the presence of a baby changes the atmosphere? Everyone smiles! And we all have the tendency to place great expectations on the child.

> So, now in our Advent preparations, let's thank God again for the mystery of birth and the miracle of new life in Jesus Christ.

Power point

Christ is the world's Light, He and none other.

Things to consider or discuss

- What hopes and expectations did your parents have for you?
- Who do you consider brings light and joy into your family or community and how?
- If you have had a child, how did that birth affect your attitudes and lifestyle?
- Which of the given names to the son in Isaiah's prophecy means the most to you and why?
- Which of these names do you think would best be understood by non-Christians?

Prayer

Advent God,
We meet to be inspired by your promised coming,
To learn your will through people who speak out for justice,
To see your power in people who bring light to others,
To find your truth from people who point to your light.
Be with us, Immanuel; the God who comes close.

Simon Walkling[1]

Pray for others

Pray for those who feel unable to break out of their gloom
   for those who are guilty of oppression
   for those you know who are dreading the approach of Christmas
   for babies being born around the world as you have been
     reading this
   for new parents
   for agencies striving for justice and peace.

Meditation

Come, thou long expected Jesus
Born to set thy people free,
From our fears and sins release us,
Let us find our rest in thee.

Israel's strength and consolation
Hope of all the earth thou art,
Dear desire of every nation,
Joy of every longing heart.

Born thy people to deliver,
Born a child and yet a King,
Born to reign in us for ever,
Now thy gracious kingdom bring.

Charles Wesley, 1707–88

2 DEC

New world vision

Television documentaries have brought the fascinations of wildlife into our homes. In comfort and safety we watch as lions attack and devour their prey, bears prowl through rubbish bins, and elegantly marked snakes shoot out their tongues into the camera.

We know more about mammals, reptiles and insects than any previous generation; we know how dangerous some can be. But how far do we equate knowledge with wisdom and understanding? In our passage for today, Isaiah prophesies the Messiah will be a judge and will turn our world order upside down. God's kingdom will be safe, His people will live in peace and be able to enjoy life.

Bible reading
Isaiah 11:1–9

Context
One of the criticisms levelled against the Old Testament is that it has far too many gory battles; too much disaster, vengeance and heartache. Well, that was how it was – and still is for millions today. Isaiah surveyed the destruction and agony of his time and recognised the cause and effect.

All that befell 'the House of David' was the consequence of Israel's kings relying on their own power and might and ignoring the power of God. One of the great themes of the Old Testament is the warning 'Do not forget your God'. Isaiah delivers his second Messianic vision to the people. We can almost hear the passion of the man as he declares the joy of a new world. The Spirit of the Lord will be on this ruler and values of the world will be superseded with God's kingdom values.

Jesus quoted similar words from Isaiah 61, when, at the beginning of His ministry, He spoke in the synagogue at Nazareth (Luke 4:2–4).

Reflection
A few months ago, I needed to attack an over-sized rubber plant before it pushed its way through the ceiling. I pruned it in half,

fearing for its life, but the plant has taken on a new lease of life and sent out seven strong shoots. Biblical writers often used the imagery of birds, plants and animals to illustrate moral, social and political truth, and once more we meet a reference to King David – naming his father Jesse. Not only does Isaiah speak of a ruler who will rule with wisdom and compassion for the poor, but the vision also implies a new kind of paradise. The whole of creation would be at peace – no more fear, no more violence, but a co-operation and interdependence which would flourish by God's direct guidance.

> **Look at where your food has come from today and pray for God's peace in the countries on the labels.**

Power point

God says: 'I am Immanuel, I am God-with-you. I am one who's not going to give you good advice from a safe distance. I enter the fiery furnace with you.'

Desmond Tutu in an Advent message to the Church in South Africa

Things to consider or discuss

- Consider people who are working overseas with aid organisations and think about how much they have given up to be there.
- Discuss the benefits of giving to a *local* charity.
- How do you deal with aggressiveness?
- In what ways do you have to exercise self-control in order to maintain peace?
- When Jesus spoke about the world not understanding the peace He gives, what do you think He meant?
- Compare Isaiah 11:5 with Ephesians 6:10–17.

Prayer

Lord, at times life seems so unfair,
I see things happening and I just don't understand:
Forgive me for making harsh judgments on those around me and those in the news;
I pray for Your Spirit of wisdom and understanding.
Thank You for the glimpses of this world as a paradise

and fill my heart today with all that is good, kind and beautiful.
I make this prayer in the name of Jesus, the Saviour of the world. Amen.

Pray for others

Pray for those who have to make life and death judgments
  for the innocent victims of violence
  for the work of The Red Cross, Médecin Sans Frontiéres,
      Oxfam, Christian Aid, Mercy Ships and similar charities
  for those who work for animal welfare
  for those working to conserve our planet.

Meditation

'All shall be well, and all shall be well and all manner of things shall be well.'

Mother Julian of Norwich

3 DEC

The glory of the Lord

Have you written all your Christmas cards? And what kind of cards will you be sending? You may have had some difficulty, amongst all the penguins, reindeers, puddings and snowmen, to find cards with Christian symbolism. In this preparation period of Advent it is both a privilege and a challenge to look closely at the message we send and to ensure that our Christmas becomes truly Christ-centred.

Bible reading

Isaiah 35

Context

Until chapter 35, most of Isaiah has been rampant condemnation of all nations, Israel and Judah included. The old phrase 'hellfire and brimstone' comes to mind at the prophet's rantings on behalf of the Lord God. The vision in this chapter now becomes a beautiful glimpse of how the kingdom of God will be so

totally, overwhelmingly wonderful that everything in creation
will be renewed and will rejoice. All the distress of the previous
pronouncements are seen in the light of the promise of a coming
Saviour, God's Messiah. Just take yourself back some 26 centuries
– tune your ear to the music of life, prosperity and gladness. Feel the
longing for transformation both in creation and in spiritual terms.

Reflection

No Christmas preparation is complete for me without hearing a
performance of Handel's *Messiah*. Much of the text is taken from
various parts of the book of Isaiah and it is, for me, a truly glorious
work where both words and music blend in sheer joyous praise. As
you reflect on these words from Isaiah, remember how Jesus took
images of the Galilean countryside to press home His message of
salvation. Remember, too, how in His ministry He opened the eyes
of the blind (Mark 10:46–52); how He told His disciples not to be
afraid (John 14:27) and how He spoke of His joy being complete in
them, His closest friends (John 15:11).

In the back of your diary or in a small, very private notebook, write
down how you see the glory of God, and how it makes you feel.

Power point

'For God, who said, "Let light shine out of darkness," made his light
shine in our hearts to give us the light of the knowledge of the glory
of God in the face of Christ.'

(2 Cor. 4:6)

Things to consider or discuss

- For what circumstances today do you need to hear those words:
  'Be strong, do not fear'?
- Discuss the meaning of the highway to Isaiah's contemporaries,
  and compare Matthew 3:1–3.
- Civil wars have destroyed the fertile land in many countries; think
  about how productive those countries could be if peace and
  justice were restored.

- 'There are none so blind as those who won't see.' What justification for this statement have you experienced?

Prayer

Lord, I pray for peace.
I long for the restoration of the world as You intended it.
In my preparations for Your coming help me to realise that not only do You come to my heart but one day You will come in glory and, as the prophets foretold, Your kingdom will never end.
For Yours is the kingdom, the power and
the glory, for ever and ever.
Amen.

Pray for others

Pray for those who are blind and unable to enjoy creation's beauty
for those who need help to walk
for those who cannot hear music, laughter, the voice of a
   loved one
for all suffering from drought and famine
for those who hear carols in residential homes and hospitals
for everyone following this study, that we may be surprised by
the joy of our Lord.

Meditation

For the beauty of the earth, for the beauty of the skies,
For the love which from our birth over and around us lies;

For the beauty of each hour of the day and of the night,
Hill and vale, and tree and flower, sun and moon, and stars
of light:

Father, unto Thee we raise
This our sacrifice of praise.

F.S. Pierpoint, 1835–1917

4 DEC

Jeremiah's voice of hope

Because we are so familiar with the Bible as 'a written book', we often overlook the fact that the prophets were far more 'preachers' than 'writers'. Their voices were heard more than their words taken down. Jeremiah's ministry covered some 40 years, and his story is one of rejection and misery. Yet however much Jeremiah suffered, he bravely continued to be a voice for the Lord God against the sin and apostasy of his time.

Bible reading
Jeremiah 23:1–6

Context
After the kings David and Solomon there had been a rapid decline in religious integrity and the epitaph for most kings who succeeded the idealised period of Solomon's rule was 'he did what was evil in the sight of the Lord'! They had been bad shepherds of the people and had cared for themselves rather than their flock. (This theme of shepherding has remained dominant in Jewish and Christian thinking.) As the nation had turned further away from the Lord God, so they had suffered disasters. In this passage Jeremiah prophesies that one day there would be a King who would reign with justice. A King would come from David's fallen dynasty and the days of fear and oppression would end. Even though Solomon built the Temple in Jerusalem and his reign brought stability and relative peace, it was David who was the national hero. Therefore, it was natural that the nation focused their longing for God's Messiah, the good and righteous King, to come from David's lineage.

Reflection
The people in Jeremiah's time were pretty discouraged – things had turned pear-shaped – but even so, they busied themselves with every distraction to avoid God's word. They were cynical about their rulers – a cynicism shared today, whether for people in government or in vast and powerful companies. We too may feel

trapped in the cycle of the rich get richer and the poor get poorer, or at best, those with influence will inevitably look after themselves. Human nature does not change over the centuries – but neither does the unshakeable faith of men and women who speak God's truth regardless of the consequences. Today, with society biting its nails over so many contentious issues, it may still feel as though no one is listening to God's voice. But do not give up – Christians must speak out against crime, corruption, oppression and violence with the vision of how God wants the world to be.

> For a glimpse at how prophets were treated, look at Hebrews 11:36–38.

Power point
Jesus said: 'I will see you again and you will rejoice, and no-one will take away your joy' (John 16:22).

Things to consider or discuss
- In what ways should we expect greater integrity from those in positions of power?
- Try to imagine how Jesus would have been taught about King David.
- This passage in Jeremiah speaks of both hope and judgment. How do these two words fit into our experience today?
- Think about another aspect of leadership apart from shepherd and sheep.
- Remember Jeremiah's faithfulness – can you be like that?

Prayer
Dear Lord, You are my shepherd,
I feel safe in Your love.
So many temptations would call me away from Your care,
it would be easy to make excuses for sliding away,
but Lord, keep me in Your like-minded flock so that
together, we will follow You,
through ups and downs,

twists and turns,
in paths of righteousness and peace. Amen.

Pray for others

Pray for young people who have been led astray into addictive habits

for those witnessing their faith in dangerous situations
for national and international leaders
for believers surrounded by non-believers at home and at work.
Give thanks for all who are lifting their voices in prayer today.

Meditation

Meditate on Psalm 23, a psalm of David.
Give thanks for the comfort it has given to millions of people.
Ask yourself what this psalm meant to Jesus.
What does it mean to you?
You may have come across some modern settings – do they relate to your situation better?

5 DEC

Songs of praise

Many years ago I was in the crowd for a television outside broadcast of favourite hymns. Unforeseen technical difficulties prolonged the recording and people began to feel – and look – fed up! Up bobbed one of the programme staff to the rescue, to engage us with mild aerobics to bring back the smiles ... the final programme looked perfect.

Bible reading

Psalm 100

Context

The book of 150 psalms is the hymnbook of the Bible. Hymns of despair, vengeance, contrition, joy and praise – the psalm writers have plumbed the depths and risen to the heights of human experience. They are profoundly moving in their honesty and openness to God and I find it quite thrilling that Jesus knew these same psalms. Many were written by King David, some were used for special occasions and some especially for pilgrimage to the Temple in Jerusalem. Psalm 100 is thought to have been the liturgy for entering the Temple. As you read these ancient words, imagine that you have saved long and hard for this journey, you have planned and waited and now you have arrived ... this is a holy place.

Reflection

Well, if you are looking for a politically correct psalm, this is it! It's a song to, and for, everyone; a spontaneous outpouring of worship and a splendid expression for us in this time of Advent. Many people who never normally go to church, will be welcomed into carol services, Christingle services and nativity plays with their family or friends, children and grandchildren – it's almost like a pilgrimage. The story and the song is for everyone. And have you ever heard a parent come away from such a service who hasn't enjoyed it? A significant difference to the atmosphere in worship creeps in at this time of year. But there is also a challenge in these words. Do we *know* the Lord is God? And are we willing and able to share our faith in God's everlasting love with young and old? When our faith is fired with thanksgiving and praise, there is no need for the manufactured smile – our joy will be real.

Power point

'... make music to the Lord with the harp, with the harp and the sound of singing, with trumpets and the blast of the ram's horn – shout for joy before the Lord, the King' (Psa. 98:5–6).

Prayer

Lord, forgive me for my half-hearted approach to Advent,
please help me to begin over again –
I want this Christmas to be special.
I want to open my heart to receive Your coming
and face the new year in humility and obedience.
I know that I am going to fail ... many times,

but I pray for the strength to persevere.
Give me a song in my heart for today. Amen.

Pray for others
Pray for all teachers and ministers of religion
    for children practising carols and nativity plays
    for children too ill to sing
    for those who have been made orphans by HIV/Aids
    for those who care for children in homes and orphanages
    for the elderly in residential care
    for those who care at home for the elderly and those frail in mind
      or spirit.

Things to consider or discuss
- In what ways has our familiarity with Jesus' coming into the world dulled our response?
- Why do you think it is always easier to judge other people than ourselves?
- What area of your faith would you really like to put into action?
- What words about God's love have you heard and remembered which have made a difference to the way you live?
- Compare a secular love-song with the words of Psalm 100.

Meditation
    Lord, make me an instrument of your peace,
    Where there is hatred, let me sow love;
    Where there is injury, pardon,
    Where there is doubt, faith,
    Where there is despair, hope,
    Where there is darkness, light;
    And where there is sadness, joy.
                The traditional prayer of St. Francis

6 DEC

Small beginnings

It is worth remembering that the greatest of cities began with the first few buildings – and the greatest intellectual minds had to learn to tie shoelaces. The King of kings came into our world as a baby – God uses small beginnings for His great purpose.

Bible reading
Micah 5:2–5

Context
The book of Micah is an extraordinary composition of classical Hebrew poetry. In standard prophet mode, each of the three main sections of the book begin with the words 'Hear' or 'Listen' as Micah addresses the people of Judea and Israel with a catalogue of their sins: fraud, theft, greed, debauchery, oppression, hypocrisy, heresy, injustice, extortion and lying, murder – and more! Quite a list for seven small chapters. But Micah also describes God's tender love and forgiveness when people turn to Him and act justly. The overwhelming flavour of this book may be ruin and disaster for those who pervert faith, but embedded in this poetry we find the little town of Bethlehem named as the birthplace for God's Messiah.

Reflection
Once again the voice of the prophet declares that the rule of God's Messiah will bring justice and peace. To his listeners, this must have sounded a somewhat empty promise in the face of all the perverted religious practices and general injustice. This is an ongoing dilemma for Christians, for we believe in the resurrection and Christ's victory over sin and death but we are still faced with the daily problems mentioned by Micah. How do we come to terms with the gift of peace from the One who was with God and was God before time began? How do we embrace the joy of God's coming in Jesus Christ whilst trouble and suffering is a daily fact? We must take heart and not be discouraged at our insignificance – David was but a boy shepherd when God told the prophet Samuel to anoint him king.

When Jesus was born, Bethlehem was but a small town – today it is world-famous.

Power point
'Be glad and rejoice with all your heart …
The LORD, the King of Israel, is with you;
never again will you fear any harm.' (Zeph. 3:14–15)

Things to consider or discuss
- Bethlehem became home to Ruth when she married Boaz; it was the home of Jesse, David, Joseph the carpenter's forbears and the birthplace of Jesus. Suggest reasons why there is no mention of Jesus ever returning to Bethlehem in His ministry.
- What was the most difficult thing to learn to do as you were growing up? For example tying shoelaces, spelling, times-tables …
- The Gospel writer, Matthew, set great store by Jesus' genealogy. How far can you trace your family tree?
- Describe the smallest town or village you have lived in.
- What is your impression of Bethlehem today?

Prayer
Lord, we hear You calling us to listen,
urging us towards justice and bidding us to be a light for the nations.
But we fail, and we know why we fail:
we do not carry Your teaching in our hearts;
we are preoccupied with other business;
we fear reproach and worry what others will say.
We are sorry …
Simon Walkling[2]

Pray for others
Pray for those living in Bethlehem today
for those who will not be at home for Christmas for different
reasons: in prison
        in hospital
        at work
        homeless
        serving in the Forces, etc.

Meditation

O holy child of Bethlehem, descend to us, we pray
Cast out our sin, and enter in;
Be born in us today.
We hear the Christmas angels the great glad tidings tell:
O come to us, abide with us,
Our Lord Immanuel.

Phillips Brooks, 1835–93

7 DEC

Song of hope

The voice we hear today is all the more challenging because
Zechariah the priest has been voiceless for several months. Denied
the natural and automatic means of communication, we can only
imagine his frustrations, yet it seems that through this period of
enforced silence he has deepened his relationship with God.

Bible reading

Luke 1:67–79

Context

Luke tells us about Zechariah and Elizabeth in unexpected detail in
the opening verses of his Gospel but, as he tells us, he has carefully
investigated everything! So we know that Zechariah and Elizabeth
were both descended from priestly clans; Zechariah served his term
at the Temple in Jerusalem, and therefore had high standing in
the community. They were no longer 'young things' and Gabriel's
announcement had left Zechariah literally speechless. It's interesting
to note that the people immediately realised something out of
the ordinary had happened to their priest and we detect an air of
bewilderment and awe. The normal outcome of this story would be
for the son to be called Zechariah, like his father, and for him to also
serve as a priest in the Temple – but we know God had a new role,
and a new name, for the boy. John is a shorter form of Jehohanan,
meaning Jehovah's gift.

Reflection

Usually we are flying about our daily routine and do not even notice the sun has come up – except that we can turn off the electric light – but I shall never forget the first time I sat silently waiting to see the sun rise over the Sea of Galilee. It was a truly spiritual experience for, unable to look into the sun, I looked at the transformation to the water and the hills – the morning light brought everything alive. As a priest, Zechariah was steeped in the longing for God's Messiah and now, in his own son, he foresaw the final preparations for the Messiah. If you read this 'song' again, there are a few things you might find you had overlooked. Yes, we have the reference to David, but this is a song of hope without vengeance. It is an acknowledgement that only by preparation will people be able to see the new dawn which will bring peace. God's peace is not just absence of conflict but the Greek words mean 'everything which makes for the highest possible good' – or, as Jesus was to describe it, 'life in all its fullness'. This is transforming joy.

Power point

'Be joyful in hope, patient in affliction, faithful in prayer' (Rom. 12:12).

Things to consider or discuss

- Do you find silence a positive or negative experience?
- Zechariah's song mentions 'salvation from our enemies'. Does this include the internal voices which pull us away from God? If so, what form does the 'enemy' take in your own life?
- How are your preparations going for this Christmas season?
- How are your spiritual preparations going?
- What do you think is the most important thing to do today?

Prayer

O living God, as we wait in these dark days for Your coming,
Silent, yearning, expectant,
Hope flickering but alight,
Place in our hands the lamps of truth and love and courage,
That we may stand firm,
And strive with those powers that rise in darkness

That the desires of all our hearts
May be fulfilled in Jesus Christ our Redeemer.

Jim Cotter[3]

Pray for others

Pray for those desperately longing to conceive
for those involved in post-natal care in your area
for support groups where children are born with multiple
problems
for parents who feel they cannot cope.
Give thanks for nurseries and playgroups
for those who cared for you as a child.

Meditation

All my hope on God is founded;
He doth still my trust renew.
Me through change and chance he guideth,
Only good and only true.
God unknown,
He alone calls my heart to be his own.

Human pride and earthly glory
Sword and crown betray our trust;
What with care and toil we fashion,
Tower and temple, fall to dust
But God's power
Hour by hour,
Is my temple and my tower.

Based on Joachim Neander, 1650–1680

Suggestions for Group Work for Week 1

Bible reading
The Leader begins with reading Isaiah 9:1–7.

Prayer
Ask one of the members to choose and read one of the prayers from the week.

Brainstorm
Have pen and paper so that each member can write down the list you make as a group (to be kept in the back of the Advent book).

List: the 9 fruits of the Spirit
        8 consumer temptations
        7 'must-do' things before Christmas
        6 favourite carols
        5 important people in your life
        4 titles given to the Messiah in the reading
        3 situations to pray for
        2 prophecies about the coming kingdom
        1 main goal for Advent

The list should take no longer than 20 minutes to compile.
Compare the 'must-do's' with the fruit of the Spirit.
End by praying for the situations mentioned and committing yourselves to the goals.
This material may appear at first glance frivolous, but some very interesting and relevant aspects of faith in action will arise.
You could each bring something next week which, for you personally, symbolises the meaning of Christ's coming into our world.

---

1. Simon Walkling, *Seasons & Celebrations* (NCEC, 1996).

2. Ibid.

3. Jim Cotter: *Prayer in the Morning* (Cairns Publication).

The Joy that Jesus Brings ...

8 DEC

Pay attention!

Does your mind ever wander? Do you ever listen to something and then are unable to remember exactly what has been said? The phrase 'pay attention' does not have exclusive classroom use! As someone I used to know would say, 'I have a good forgettery', and, just because we feel familiar with the story of our Saviour's birth doesn't mean we have perfect recall. Quite a lot of our perception of Jesus is subconsciously coloured by centuries-old art and Victorian carols. So, let's pretend we are hearing about Jesus for the first time ...

Bible reading
Hebrews 1:6–9; 2:1–4

Context
Probably this letter was written to second-generation Christians, circa AD 80. But who wrote it? Scholarly suggestions have named Barnabas, Apollos and even a joint effort by Aquila and Priscilla. However, the enigma remains – the author is anonymous. Even so, the letter contains two particular points relevant to our Advent devotions. The group of Christians receiving this letter were faced with a double emphasis on Jesus' unique birth. This wasn't just another prophet; this letter contains bold, unequivocal teaching about God's Son. Ninety-nine per cent of the epistles ignore our Lord's actual birth, but this writer appears to make direct reference to the angels' joy in sharing the news with the shepherds outside

Bethlehem. This is no light comment – it was a truth the writer was prepared to die for. It is a message that needs our careful attention, too; our spiritual growth depends upon it.

Reflection

I love receiving letters. No matter how miraculous emails are, for me there is nothing quite like the excitement of picking up post dropped through the letter-box. When I recognise the writing on the envelope, I know instantly who has sent it and where it has come from. I expect in those biblical days, pre-printing, pre-widespread literacy, it was even more exciting for first-century Christians to receive news and teaching from the apostles – maybe they were living in Corinth, Cyprus, Alexandria, Rome, or in one of the many small towns and villages where just a nucleus of converts waited for encouragement.

Have you ever paused to imagine the courage, enthusiasm and charisma that compelled those first evangelists to testify far and wide to the love and joy of Jesus Christ?

Power point

Paul wrote: 'Rejoice in the Lord always. I will say it again: Rejoice!' (Phil. 4:4).

Things to consider or discuss

- Think about the disciples travelling with the 'good news' – measure your own enthusiasm with that of the Early Church.
- Why is it so difficult to pay attention?
- What is the best news you have ever received?
- Write a letter to an imaginary community and try to explain that Jesus Christ can make a difference to their lives.
- Ask yourself: have you enough love and joy in the Lord Jesus to sustain you in the face of prejudice or intimidation?
- Is there a letter you need to write? Don't put it off any longer.

Prayer

Give thanks for all forms of twenty-first-century communications
> for telephones … including mobile phones!
> for radio, television and DVDs
> for international satellite links
> for emails and videos
> for letters, cards and books
> for the voices of those we love.

Pray for others

Pray for journalists in dangerous and difficult places; for camera crew in disaster areas
> for artists
> for writers
> for musicians
> for actors
> for dancers.

Meditation

> Life and light and joy are found in the presence of the Lord:
> Life with richest blessing crowned,
> Light from many fountains poured –
> Life, and light and holy joy – none can darken, or destroy.
>> Charles Edward Mudie, 1818–90

9 DEC

Party time

This time of year is party time! Office parties, company Christmas lunches, school Christmas parties – the great competition to 'ding-dong merrily' sometimes with rather tense, contrived enjoyment. Gatherings can be great fun and shared celebrations help to forge friendship between strangers; however, successful parties take a lot of thought and organisation – and the host/hostess can only truly relax properly when it is all over!

Bible reading
John 2:1–11

Context

Unlike our parties, ancient Near-Eastern wedding celebrations could go on for days! In the midst of a pretty harsh existence, a wedding would be a momentous and joyful occasion to be shared with as many people as possible. Most times we only register this story as the first of Jesus' miracles, but as always with the disciple John, this is a many-layered account. Mary, Jesus and the disciples had all been invited, which seems to indicate they were close friends or even relatives of the couple, especially when we realise that Mary had authority to give orders to the servants in the house. Hospitality was a sacred duty in those times and wine was essential for any feast. Ancient rabbis had a saying: 'Without wine there is no joy!' To run out of wine therefore was social disaster and humiliation.

Reflection

I used to have a little cross-stitch picture with the words:

> *Happiness is a butterfly, which when pursued is just beyond your grasp.*
> *But if you will sit down quietly, it will alight upon you.*

It's surprising how things in the background of life, by their very familiarity, become part of our subconscious. This Victorian nugget of wisdom was only a picture when I was a child, but as an adult, I can see the truth in those words. The pursuit of happiness began with Adam and Eve as they ate the forbidden fruit and today everyone is hurtling after happiness as though it is obligatory to 'have a good time' *all* the time. Our life in Jesus helps us to find contentment and fulfilment in and through daily events. Joy comes from within.

In this miracle, Jesus turns the situation around. Is this what He is waiting to do in your life? It may be time to slow down a bit and give yourself the opportunity for His Spirit to alight upon you.

Power point
His mother said: 'Do whatever he tells you.'

Things to consider or discuss
- When did you last go to a party?
- What kind of people would you try to avoid inviting to a celebration?
- How do you think the disciples interpreted this 'sign'?
- In chapter 1 of his Gospel, John names the first disciples who would have been with Jesus in Cana – look and see who they were.
- Which is the greater miracle – that Jesus turned water into wine or that Jesus, the Son of God, was present to enjoy ordinary family festivities?
- Why is Christmas the most hospitable time of the year?

Prayer
Jesus, Lord and Saviour, come into my life and turn the water of my mundane routine into the wine of new life in You. Thank You for those You have given me to love and those who love me. Open my eyes to the priceless gift of family and friends. In these days of Advent help me to treasure opportunities to celebrate Your coming into the world.

Pray for others
Pray for those who have been married this year
    for marriages falling apart
    for those who are divorced
    for children with multiple 'parents'
    for grandparents who have lost touch with grandchildren
    for those who abuse alcohol
    for the work of Alcoholics Anonymous

Meditation
'Then celebrate the Feast … to the LORD your God by giving a freewill offering in proportion to the blessings the LORD your God has given you. And rejoice before the LORD your God … you, your sons and daughters, your menservants and maidservants,

the Levites in your towns, and the aliens, the fatherless and the
widows living among you.'
(Deut. 16:10–11)

Come on – let's celebrate!

10 DEC

Celebration of love

In his meditation 'The Fear of Love', Frank Topping wrote:

Forgive me if I am afraid to give a little time, a little laughter,
 a little joy.
I am afraid of love because loving is giving and I am afraid of
the cost.

The frantic commercial hype can entrap us in a consumer hamster-
wheel of rushing around, exhaustion, disappointment and debt. This
is not what true 'giving' is about.

Surely, 'giving' is a response to 'loving' and love is the greatest of
all God's gifts.

Bible reading
1 Corinthians 13

Context
Corinth was a 'New Town' in Paul's day and, as such, it has a
contemporary feel for today. The Greek city had been destroyed
about 150 BC and more or less abandoned for a century. Then
the Romans rebuilt Corinth, re-igniting its commercial heart, its
athletic reputation, as well as its reputation for the seamier side of
life! Between the lines of Paul's letter you can detect the bustling
brashness of the Corinthians which had sadly entered their church
community. Paul wrote to counteract the arrogance of Corinthian
material and spiritual *show*, to bring them to understand that there
are more important values than 'fastest', 'richest' or 'brainiest'. They

needed to find *God's* values which could never be destroyed and which everyone could embrace.

Reflection

Why do people say 'Christmas is a time for the children'? Does adulthood imply that we have moved beyond appreciating the love that came down at Christmas? What an empty festival Christmas would be if this were true. Don't let us downgrade the mystery and miracle of Christ's human birth by reducing it to a children's entertainment – something we grow out of. The baby Jesus was no toy and there is nothing remotely glitzy, childish or jovial about the manner of His death on a cross. Jesus Christ came into the real world for love of you and me and the blessing of that love is something we shall never be too grown-up to receive.

Power point

'Love never fails' (1 Cor. 13:8).

Things to consider and discuss
- Try to be brutally honest here: Which presents do you give as a duty and which as a loving response?
- Read verses 4–6 again and put the name of Jesus in the place of the word 'love'.
- Dare to read verses 4–6 again with your own name in the place of the word 'love' and meditate on the outcome.
- What childhood memories of Christmas make you feel good?
- Consider the statement: 'Christians are too fond of adoring the baby and the cross but do not spend enough time on the teaching in the middle.'
- In what ways does love grow cold?

Prayer

Lord of Love, I pray today for all those who feel unloved, neglected and lonely in the midst of this family-orientated season. Lord, help us to know we are bound together in Your family, and in our caring for one another, may we grow in the knowledge and love of Your Son, Jesus Christ our Lord.

Pray for others

Pray for those who have no blood-ties of family
  for mothers who gave their babies for adoption
  for parents whose children are in care
  for those who are so badly affected by abuse they are afraid
    to love
  for the caring agencies who seek to build a brighter future for
    children and families.
Give thanks for the happy families you know.

Meditation

Love divine, all loves excelling,
Joy of heaven to earth come down.
Fix in us thy humble dwelling
All thy faithful mercies crown.
Jesu, thou art all compassion,
Pure, unbounded love thou art;
Visit us with thy salvation,
Enter every trembling heart.

Charles Wesley, 1707–88

11 DEC

Nativity for all

Just pause for a moment to register the unique impact of the nativity.

This was God's initiative, the Almighty Creator God moving in human history.

The birth of a baby boy, born over 2,000 years ago, is still celebrated by young and old the world over; celebrated by people of Christian faith, other faiths and professing no faith. The story is retold in hundreds of languages and even our system of dating in most parts of the world stems from that one birth. Jesus – Saviour of the *world*.

Bible reading
Matthew 1:18–25

Context

Whereas Luke gives the birth narratives a definite slant to Mary's story, Matthew brings Joseph into higher profile. Joseph is hardly mentioned anywhere else, but in these verses we glimpse an honourable and devout Jew who was a considerate and loving husband at a time when these virtues could not be taken for granted.

Notice too how Matthew declares that Mary had conceived by the Holy Spirit; the embryo in her womb was God's miracle. As a devout Jew, Joseph would have been waiting for the prophesied Messiah, the longing of every Jew to see God's Anointed bring about the new order of peace and justice. Think what a significant name the angel gave to Joseph for the baby, the Greek equivalent of the Hebrew Joshua – literally meaning God's salvation. To suggest Joseph was pole-axed by the prospect of such responsibility is the understatement of the year.

Reflection

St Francis certainly began something when he directed the re-enactment of Jesus' birth by the Assisi villagers. The visual impact of that first nativity play loses nothing as each generation gives its own interpretation of the miraculous event. Last year, white tutu-clad budding ballerinas leapt into the pulpit in a froth of tulle and tinsel, all eager to proclaim 'Glad tidings of great joy' and a huge toy sheep skulked for days in the church vestry before returning 'home'. But I shall never forget a nativity performed in a psychiatric hospital. 'Mary' was a shy 50-year-old and 'Joseph' was in a wheelchair. The 'kings' and 'shepherds' had to be coaxed onto the stage and positioned by the caring hands of nurses, yet their reverence moved me to tears. 'Mary' ecstatically cradled the doll in her arms, looked up and beamed: 'I wish my mummy could see me now!' It was an Immanuel moment – we all felt (the presence of) God with us.

Power point

Paul wrote: 'He [Jesus] died for all' (2 Cor. 5:15).

Things to consider or discuss

- With people who have a different level of understanding, how do we share the love and joy of Jesus?

- What do you think are the advantages of adults performing the nativity?
- What is your picture of Joseph?
- If God is the Creator of life, how does that influence your view on the sanctity of life?
- What do 'names' mean to you and are there certain 'names' which create a picture in your mind; like 'Mary'?
- In what ways has somebody else's faith helped you change your attitude?

Prayer

Loving heavenly Father, thank You that Jesus came into the world for everyone. Thank You that I don't have to be brilliant, famous or rich to know His saving love.

Thank You that the language of a smile, a hug or a kiss is universally understood.

Show me how much I can receive from the trusting faith of others. I pray in the name of Jesus. Amen.

Pray for others

Pray for all staff in psychiatric hospitals
    for community psychiatric nurses
    for residential care staff
    for God's children who need special understanding, care and support
    for parents who cannot cope with the needs of their children.
Give thanks for the dedicated research that continually markets new and better medication.

Meditation

Then God sent an angel from heaven so high,
To certain poor shepherds in fields where they lie,
And bade them no longer in sorrow to stay
Because that our Saviour was born on this day:

Then presently after the shepherds did spy
A number of angels that stood in the sky;

They joyfully talked and sweetly did sing,
'To God be all glory, our heavenly King.'

Traditional carol

12 DEC

Communicating the good news

Communication – communication – communication. That could be
the mantra for our age! At the touch of a mouse, a bounced beam
from a satellite, or reception of invisible airwaves, we have global
communication. How fantastic! But all these miracles have been
available for discovery since the dawn of creation – these are not
human *creations* but human *discoveries*. Our awesome God has
created all things.

Bible reading
Matthew 28:16–20

Context
These last verses in Matthew's Gospel leave us in no doubt that Jesus
is the Messiah.

Right at the beginning Matthew goes into the genealogy to prove
Jesus a descendant of King David; and tells how the Magi come to
Jerusalem searching for the one 'who has been born king of the
Jews' (2:2). Later on, it is Matthew who records Pilate asking Jesus,
'Are you the King of the Jews?' (27:11), to which Jesus answers, 'Yes.'

As Matthew comes to the end of his Gospel, he records our
Saviour's solemn commission to the disciples. Jesus tells His disciples
that He has authority over all the world; His mission is now handed
to the disciples. Matthew, the Jewish tax-collector, bursts the bounds
of religious acceptability to include the whole world in God's grace
– and that means 'Gentiles'. The prophesied Immanuel would be an
eternal presence – mind-blowing!

Reflection
Matthew records what he believed to be Jesus' most important last

words to the disciples. Put in modern terms – *Get out there and spread the news.*

For many years I lived in Cornwall, the county in which a modern miracle was pioneered. On 12 December 1901, Guglielmo Marconi used a spark gap transmitter to send the first transatlantic message from Poldhu in Cornwall to Newfoundland. This successful experiment was the forerunner to all the modern communication systems we take for granted today. But the disciples had managed without sophisticated electronic devices, they transmitted the good news of the Messiah by the greatest and most powerful means of communication ever – the voice.

They dispersed throughout the known world to tell everyone of Jesus Christ, the Saviour of the world.

Power point

'But you will receive power when the Holy Spirit comes on you; and you will be my witnesses ... to the ends of the earth.'
(Acts 1:8)

Things to consider or discuss

- Remind yourself of an occasion when you kept silent rather than shared your faith.
- The passage mentions doubters – who do you think they were?
- Imagine what the disciples did after Jesus had commissioned them.
- How would you have felt if you had been the wife (or relative) of one of the disciples, for instance Peter?
- Even though the disciples had seen the miracle of the resurrected Jesus, they were still unable to evangelise before Pentecost. Discuss the difference Pentecost made.

Prayer

Forgive me, Lord, that bad news remains in my mind so much more than good.

Show me how in these days of Advent I may speak of Your coming, and encourage others to hear the message of joy for the whole world.

Pray for others

Pray for inventors and communicators.
Give thanks for the inventors of radio
   of television and telephone
   for those who use the world wide web
   for all who share their faith with their children, parents,
    godparents and grandparents
   all who will hear the Christmas message over the coming days.

Meditation

   The Lord has given me a voice:
   The Lord has blessed me with people to speak to –
   The Lord has gifted others to invent means of bringing joy and
    laughter,
   Knowledge and understanding,
   The world that is so vast is made smaller by a phone-call,
   More amazing by photography,
   More precious by the birth of a baby.
   The Lord has given me birth, life and rebirth in faith.
   Blessed be the name of the Lord.

13 DEC

Take it to the Lord in prayer

One of today's most widely-read spiritual writers, Henri Nouwen, described *discipline* as the other side of *discipleship*. This came to me as a totally new thought – especially when I acknowledge discipline is an uncomfortable word at this time of year!

Bible reading

Matthew 6:25–34

Context

These words are found in the beautiful raft of teaching called The Sermon on the Mount. In this sixth chapter of Matthew's Gospel, Jesus has already been speaking about giving to the needy, and sincere fasting. In the middle has come the profound teaching on prayer with The Lord's Prayer, but joined on to these spiritual highs Jesus shows He understands that His hearers cannot hold the mountain-top experience. They were as bound up with family, home and work as we are. Jesus gently tried to move them on by directing their eyes to God's creation all around. Take a look yourself at the glorious created world around us, in the air, on the ground, below ground and in the rivers and oceans. By His own example, Jesus taught His followers to have complete reliance upon God for everything. Only by this open trust, grounded in a disciplined prayer life, do we find serenity and peace.

Reflection

From time to time I expect we are all guilty of being so anxious about a coming situation that we're unable to enjoy the present. There is much to worry about: our job, our parents and/or children, redundancy or retirement, ill health, finance ... the list is hardly begun! Worry is time-consuming as we all know but it fails to combat the pressures. It gives me great comfort to read that the people who had the incredible privilege of seeing and learning from Jesus were also first-degree worriers.

Maybe you need to ask yourself today – what exactly am I worrying about?

Then, bring those loved ones or the situations to God in prayer. As you visualise them in your mind's eye, see Jesus with His hand on the person or people concerned, and on you. By the power of the Holy Spirit you will be enabled to carry on.

Power point

Through a spiritual discipline we prevent the world from filling our lives to such an extent that there is no place left to listen. (Henri Nouwen)[1]

Things to consider or discuss

- What is worrying you at this moment?
- Discuss Jesus' upbringing and how He first learned to pray.
- Try to remember the first prayer you learned.
- Where do you find you are able to pray best?

- In what ways do you think it helps people to know they are being prayed for?
- Take a newspaper cutting and pray for a situation or person in that cutting.

Prayer

Lord, our God, eternal and wonderful,
you help those who come to you
and give hope to those who call on you.
Set our hearts and minds at peace
that we may bring our prayers to you
with confidence and joy;
through Jesus Christ our Lord. Amen.

Methodist Worship Book

Pray for others

Pray for those whose lives have been blighted by anxiety
to be gentle with someone who irritates you
for those who feel suicidal
for those suffering from breakdowns
for those who silently bear unsolvable problems
for someone you know, to find time for Jesus.

Meditation

Not a burden we bear, not a sorrow we share,
But our toil he doth richly repay;
Not a grief nor a loss, not a frown nor a cross
But is blest if we trust and obey.

But we never can prove the delights of his love
Until all on the altar we lay;
For the favour he shows and the joy he bestows
Are for them who will trust and obey.

John Henry Sammis

14 DEC

Sweet perfume ...

It's in the John Betjeman classic 'Christmas' that we find the lines 'the sweet and silly Christmas things, bath salts and inexpensive scent'. We've probably all been on the receiving end of such unwanted toiletries. However much kindness is behind them, in our individuality, we all like different things. Yet perfume is so ancient a process and, along with aromatic spices, it has its place in Scripture.

Bible reading
Matthew 26:6–13

Context
Both Matthew and Mark place this event in the house of Simon the Leper, while John in his Gospel recorded the event as in Lazarus' home with Mary being the woman who anointed Jesus. From this story, in three Gospels, we can trace some key facts.

Bethany must have been a regular stop for Jesus and His disciples, and Mary and Martha's home was not the only place where He received hospitality. To have the incident recorded by three evangelists shows what importance was placed on such an anointing. Why? Well, all those who heard about it would realise the twofold reference both to anointing and also to the costly ointment. The woman used a sacrificial gift to proclaim Jesus King in her eyes, but Jesus, who had predicted His immanent death, accepted it as a beautiful preparation for His burial. This tender act of love and reverence lives on wherever the gospel is told – just as Jesus said it would.

Reflection
The more we love someone, the more we want to lavish gifts on them. Years ago the papers were full of the enormous diamond that the actor Richard Burton had bought for Elizabeth Taylor – ostentatious in the extreme – but it was a gift to show the world how much he loved her. Just as in Matthew's story, there is always someone who will grumble at such extravagance! Isn't it amazing

that the Lord of lords and King of kings is waiting to receive our gift? He gave His life for us, and there is no greater love than that. Our gift is our loving response, our commitment to deepen our love and knowledge of Jesus and His teaching and to live in the world to His glory.

Power point
'Perfume and incense bring joy to the heart ...' (Prov. 27:9).

Things to consider or discuss
- Reflect on the three occasions when costly perfume was brought to Jesus: Matthew 2:11; Mark 14:3; John 19:39.
- Discuss how different aromas evoke certain memories.
- Discuss the rise in popularity for scented candles and oils.
- For what present or deed would you like to be remembered?
- Imagine you were a friend of Martha and Mary, what would be your reaction on hearing what had happened to Jesus?
- In what ways do we proclaim Jesus Lord and King?

Prayer
Lord, teach me that there is joy in giving as well as receiving; may I always be aware that, even if I do not like or need the gift, somebody bothered to remember me.
I pray for generosity of spirit and a grateful heart.
Above all, I praise you for the love which surrounds me each and every day.
Bless and guide me in these days of Advent preparation, for Jesus Christ's sake, Amen.

Pray for others
Pray for children in Eastern European orphanages who will receive Christmas presents from churches in other countries
    for those who check, pack and transport the gifts
    for the international work of the Salvation Army
    for those who cannot afford presents
    for those working in the perfume industry, in chocolate factories and florists
    for people who always grumble.

Meditation

What can I give him, poor as I am?
If I were a shepherd I would bring a lamb.
If I were a wise man, I would do my part,
Yet what I can I give him –
Give my heart.

Christina Rossetti, 1830–94

Suggestions for Group Work Week 2

Bible reading
Matthew 6:25–34

Sharing
Having asked the group last week to bring something which, for them personally, symbolised the meaning of Christ's coming into our world, ask for people to display their item and share their thoughts.

Light a scented candle and listen to Beethoven's *Ode to Joy* or some other inspirational music.

Discussion
Either:

The daily themes through this week have been about how Jesus touched the daily lives of ordinary people – each group member may like to choose one discussion subject from each day. If there are more than seven members of the group do not worry that they may choose the same point, it will always have a different angle.

Or:

- You are writing to tell a non-Christian friend about the nativity – how would you describe it?
- Discuss the wide implications of hospitality.
- Read 1 Corinthians 13 and reflect on Joseph's love for Mary.
- If you were marooned on a desert island, which modern form of communication would you most miss and why?
- Discuss the purpose and benefits of nativity plays.
- How can we prepare to enjoy Christmas when so many people are hurting?

Prayer

End with the prayer from 9 December.

Everyone should choose a Christmas card to bring next time, and be prepared to say why you chose it and how you feel the card shows the message of Christ's birth.

1. Henri Nouwen, *Circles of Love* (Darton Longman & Todd, 1988), p.41

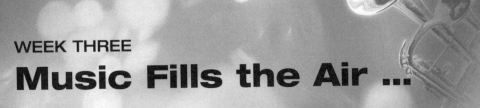

Music Fills the Air ...

15 DEC

Hark, the glad sounds!

I doubt if you have reached this far into December without hearing: 'I'm dreaming of a white Christmas …' The golden oldies trill out across the airwaves alongside other new songs competing to top the charts by Christmas. This is also the time of year for some of the most beautiful music ever written – it's a time for music in the air and a song in the heart.

Bible reading
Nehemiah 12:27–29, 40–43

Context
The books of Ezra and Nehemiah cover the initial period when the Jews returned from Exile to the ruins of their beloved holy city, Jerusalem. Cyrus, the King of Persia (present-day Iran) magnanimously returned to the Jews much of the Temple treasures which had been looted by Nebuchadnezzar when the Babylonians sacked Jerusalem in 597 BC. Today's reading records in amazing detail the ceremonial celebrations to praise God for the restoration of the city walls. Trumpets and fanfares still form part of our ceremonials – in fact it's fascinating how little the elements of national rejoicing have changed over the millennia.

Reflection

For many years I belonged to a group who went carol singing in aid of Cancer Research. Several nights before Christmas we dressed in Victorian costume and walked around the streets to various homes in the town and nearby hamlet. I doubt if we made a heavenly sound but people looked forward to our coming and to hearing the old familiar carols. One particular night we stood on the little green surrounded by cottages and sang a lilting Cornish version of 'While Shepherds ...'. People stood smiling at their front doors and others opened windows, then suddenly, in the gentle darkness, snowflakes began to fall. For one of the elderly ladies who heard us that night, it was her last Christmas on earth. I shall always remember the privilege and the fun of being part of that group of friends, singing to all of our Saviour's birth.

Power point

'Come, let us sing for joy to the LORD (Psa. 95:1).

Things to consider or discuss

- Which is your favourite carol and why?
- Which carol do you really hope you never sing again – and why?
- What part does music play in your life at this time of year?
- If you have been to a ceremonial occasion, what impressed you most?
- Consider the large part music played in ancient worship, and think of the music in your local church.
- Reflect on this statement: Words touch the heart but music touches the soul.

Prayer

Lord, thank You for the great gift of music. Thank You for all the songs that bring joy to my heart – for the memories that certain music evokes – may I see in the enormous diversity in music the reflection of human diversity, empowered and guided by the Great Conductor. Lord, help me to keep in tune with Your will and thereby create harmony with those around me. Amen.

Pray for others

Let's give thanks for those who go out singing carols
　　in hospitals
　　in residential homes
　　in the high streets for charity.
　　Pray for those who are nearing the end of life.
　　Pray for pop 'idols' and their influence on the young.

Have a go at composing a Christmas Carol

Meditation

　　The wireless brings us songs of Christmas praise
　　From far and near;
　　And, listening, we are one with you today –
　　Friends … everywhere!
　　　　　　　　Yamamoto, a Japanese Christian leprosy sufferer

16 DEC

Is yours a Christ-centred Christmas?

In December 1908, an elderly clergyman in London sent out
Christmas postcards to his parishioners. The quaint card read:

　　　　　　with all best wishes
　　　　　　　　for
　　　　　　a happy Christmas
　　　　　and a bright new year
　　　　　　　　from
　　　　　the Vicar and Mrs Henrey.

　And the picture on the card? A photograph of the vicar!
　What a travesty of the message of our Saviour's birth! In this
season of Advent let us focus a little less upon ourselves and put
Jesus centre stage.

Bible reading
1 John 4:7–21

Context
This is John the disciple, writing from Ephesus to Christian congregations whose faith was being undermined by heretical ideas. Some of these intellectual arguments fiercely denied the Incarnation of Jesus Christ, so in this letter John, by then probably the last surviving of the original disciples, encourages the faithful to be confident and not led astray by trends and false teaching. John is clear that love is the key to all the Messiah's teaching; remember, this is the disciple who recorded Jesus' new commandment (John 13:34). A lovely story told by Jerome describes how the very ancient John would be carried into the Ephesus congregation. Too feeble to preach, he would just say, 'Little children, love one another.' Some of the people grew bored with this repetition, to which John responded: 'It is the Lord's command. If this is all you do, it is enough.'

Reflection
What is Advent all about?

I'm not thinking about the meaning of the word 'Advent', I'm looking behind the definition and trying to discover the purpose of this time and what God is saying to us through His Word. John's letter to the early Christian communities states that God sent His Son into the world to be Saviour not just of the Jews but the Saviour of the whole world. But it doesn't end there – each one of us is called to make our response to this Saviour, and our response is what can change the world. In his book, *God has a Dream*, Archbishop Emeritus Desmond Tutu wrote: 'All over this magnificent world God calls us to extend his kingdom of shalom – peace and wholeness – of justice, of goodness, of compassion, of caring and sharing, of laughter, of joy, and of reconciliation.'

Power point
Jesus said: 'For God so loved the world that he gave his one and only Son, that whoever believes in him shall not perish but have eternal life' (John 3:16).

Things to consider or discuss

- Former Archbishop Tutu is recognised as a man of peace and reconciliation; who else would you say fits that description?
- Discuss the consequences of John 13:34.
- Discuss the consequences of ignoring John 13:34.
- What do you feel God is saying to you in these Advent studies?
- Compare 1 John 4:9 with John 3:16.
- We think of John as 'the beloved disciple' – consider the impact on us when someone shows us sacrificial love.

Prayer

Lord, give me courage to stand firm in my faith. When others would question, distort or trivialise Your coming, when doubts and preoccupations cloud my mind, open my heart to hear the song of angels, to feel the joy of expectancy, to marvel that You love me. Then send me into the day to share a smile.

Pray for others

Pray for those who have been led away from the faith they once held
for families divided by faith
for those who have been damaged by loveless 'religion'
for greater understanding and dialogue between local churches
for the worldwide family of believers.

Meditation

Son of the eternal Father,
Who again in power shall come:
Cherub, seraph-hosts adorning, Swell his state, and loudly cry:
Hallelujah! Hallelujah! Hallelujah!
Praise ye him, the living Lord.

Thomas Merritt: Cornish musician, d.1908

17 DEC

Prayer, the pulse through everyday life

The words of Michel Quoist always inspire me and offer a new insight into familiar situations and habits. Here is a quote I have kept in my mind for many years: '... the silent prayer which has moved beyond words must always spring from everyday life, for everyday life is the raw material of prayer.'

Try to give yourself some still moments today to pray to God in silence.

Bible reading
John 17:13–23

Context
Can you believe Jesus is *praying for you*? These are such incredibly intimate chapters, so close to the crucifixion, and yet Jesus is concerned for His disciples who were with Him and those who would be disciples in the future. Judas had already left the group when Jesus spoke these words. Obviously they were worried and upset at the thought that He was 'going away' but Jesus told them not to worry (John 14:1) and that their grief would turn to joy (16:20). The disciples were promised that deep contentment of knowing they were unconditionally loved, and that knowledge would sustain them through everything that lay ahead.

That joy is for all believers in every time and place.

Reflection
We know that Jesus had grown up to seek a solitary place in which to pray (Mark 1:35; Luke 5:16). Just think about the noisy carpenter's shop, the constant comings and goings in the Nazareth street, the clatter of younger brothers and sisters – hardly peaceful! Jesus recognised His need of quiet prayer, a need to withdraw from the hassle and talk things through with His Father God. This was a practice our Lord encouraged His disciples to follow as we find

in Matthew's Gospel (Matt. 6:6): 'But when you pray, go into your room, close the door and pray to your Father …' Don't you find it awesome that we can turn in prayer to God, our Father, the same God and Father of our Lord Jesus? The same God to whom Mary prayed, the God who heard the prayers of the prophets, the God who was, and is, and is to be! Immortal, invisible – Holy is His name.

This almighty, loving God hears our prayers.

That lovely lady of faith, Corrie ten Boom, said: 'How little we realise the great importance of intercessory prayer. If at this moment you pray for someone, even though they are on the other side of the globe, the hand of Jesus will touch them.'

Power point

Paul wrote: 'Devote yourselves to prayer, being watchful and thankful' (Col. 4:2).

Things to consider or discuss

- Discuss the importance of praying for others.
- Reflect on your own quiet times with the Lord and how you would like to add to these times.
- When peace and quiet is impossible, how do you pray?
- What is your reaction when you feel prayers have not been answered?
- What positive experiences have you had of people praying for you?
- What is the most important thing to pray for today?
- Think about and discuss the ways in which our relationship with God and Jesus deepens by regular prayer.

Prayer

Lord Jesus Christ, we welcome you –
In weakness to find courage,
In penitence to find a new beginning,
In uncertainty to find a next step,
In loneliness to find companionship.

Lynne Chitty

Pray for others

Pray for those who never seem to have a minute for themselves
for those who feel they have nothing to contribute
for those who spend too much time on their own
for those whose every day life and routine is falling apart.
Give thanks for those who daily pray for others.

Meditation

As o'er each continent and island
The dawn leads on another day,
The voice of prayer is never silent
Nor dies the strain of praise away.

John Ellerton, 1826–93

18 DEC

Time for the children

A crowd of some 20,000 people stood for hours waiting to hear an address by Nelson Mandela. His words were not only directed at world leaders but at the children – the generation which carries hopes and dreams for a better world. Mandela, that colossus amongst 'celebrities', made time for the children.

Bible reading

Mark 10:13–16

Context

We tend to think of divorce as a relatively modern 'problem', but 2,000 years ago Pharisees were plying Jesus with questions about it. Clearly it was an issue and as Mark follows this subject matter with the touching scene of Jesus blessing the children, it implies the value Jesus put upon the stability of family life.

Family breakdown is always sad and, sometimes, inevitable, but nobody escapes these domestic traumas without scars, especially the children. Why did Jesus make so much of the children? Was it to teach the Pharisees the lessons of trust, humility, curiosity, wonder and obedience? Could it be that we need to realise there is no room in the kingdom of heaven for grudges, bitterness and self-seeking – that we only enter into that kingdom with innocence, openness and the sheer joy of being loved and accepted – just as we are.

Reflection

In the heart of the countryside, for one week each summer, it is possible to spend a day watching a drama about 'The Life of Christ'.[1] Some 200 actors enact the story of Jesus from the nativity to the resurrection, all out in the open, in a natural amphitheatre setting. The 'audience' sits on straw bales or on the ground and the mixture of fine acting, live animals and authentic costumes combine to rival Oberammagau in spiritual impact. One of the most human scenes for me was the sight of 20 to 30 excited children racing towards 'Jesus' and shouting 'Jesus! Jesus! Jesus!'

It really brought to life their innocent delight in Jesus' arrival in their village.

> In our Advent journey perhaps we need to ask ourselves – are we *thrilled* by His coming? Or is it just another Christmas?

Power point

Jesus said: 'Whoever welcomes a little child like this in my name welcomes me' (Matt. 18:5).

Things to consider or discuss

- When you are busy and tired, how do you hold on to Christ as the centre of Christmas?
- How did you feel when, as a child, someone was irritated and dismissive of your excitement?
- As a child, did you enjoy the story of Jesus' birth, and what did it mean to you?
- Consider the children abused in the sex-trade, and children made to fight in civil wars – what is our Christian duty?
- What thrills you about the coming of Jesus?
- What would you do if Jesus were coming tomorrow – to your home?

Prayer

Lord, I long to recapture a child-like trust and praying love.

In these days of Advent, help me to appreciate those who helped mould me as a child, those who told me about Jesus, my Saviour and my Friend.

Warm my heart with renewed wonder, love and praise as the familiar words and songs of this season lead me onwards towards the Bethlehem manger.

Pray for others

Pray for children who have been abandoned
    for those who are loved in adoptive homes
    for those who are loved in a foster-family
    for those who are aborted
    for children who live on the streets
    for those who are abused in the sex trade
    that the children in your family may learn to love the Lord Jesus.

Meditation

Jesus, Friend of little children, be a Friend to me;
Take my hand and ever keep me close to thee.
Teach me how to grow in goodness, daily as I grow;
Thou hast been a child, and surely, thou dost know.
Never leave me nor forsake me, ever be my Friend;
For I need thee from life's dawning to its end.

Walter J. Mathams, 1853–1931

19 DEC

The light of life

In today's Advent reading we look at one of the most frequently read passages at this time of year, but also one of the least straightforward. Yet John, the young disciple whom Jesus loved, felt these words so vital to His message that they form the famous 'Prologue' to his, the fourth and last, Gospel.

Bible reading
John 1:1–14

Context
With all the shepherds, wise men and stable images around at the
moment, just pause to reflect on how and why John ignored all
those things. One of the closest witnesses to Jesus' life, death and
resurrection, begins his Gospel with the most staggering, spiritual
declaration. Combining both the Jewish idea of the Word of God (as
in 'God said: ...') with the Greek word *Logos*, John draws a picture
of the Messiah as the embodiment of all creative power, energy,
wisdom and reason. Light was the sign of His divinity, the light
which was eternal, born into the world, into human life, by the Holy
Spirit.

By the time this fourth Gospel was committed to written form,
it seems that the Gentiles, Greek-speaking believers, heavily out-
numbered the Jewish Christians, a fact which surely influenced John
as he recorded this inspired foreword. Again, looking at the use of
Greek, the words for 'true' and 'real' are of the same root. So John
tells us that Jesus was not only real in the sense of being human but
He was spiritually real; He was – and is – Truth.

Reflection
In the hymn which could be called the anthem for Christmas, 'O
come all ye faithful', there is direct reference to this Bible reading:
'True God of true God' and 'Word of the Father now in flesh
appearing'. John wrote, with complete intellectual sincerity, the truth
as he perceived it. Jesus shared the mystery and majesty of creation –
then in human form, He brought the light of revelation into the lives
of believers. Jesus is our glimpse of God. Jesus is the prophesied
Messiah – the light of the world – and however dark the world has
been at times, His light has never been extinguished.

Belief in Jesus, our Lord, changes lives even today when people
are so desperate to find reason and fulfilment.

In his book *Desert Island Hymns*, Reverend Stephen Dawes describes his belief in Jesus: 'I believe him to be the clue to the meaning of life, the universe and everything; and that following him is what the Christian faith is about.' Are you able to say the same?

Power point
All who believe in Jesus are children of God.

Things to consider or discuss
- Consider the similarities between Genesis 1:1 and John 1:1–2.
- John's Prologue is either misguided blasphemy or revelation of eternal truth. What are the implications of his words being true?
- Think about the character of John. Jesus had called him a 'son of thunder' (Mark 3:17). How does this square in your mind with 'the beloved disciple'?
- Jesus said, 'I am the light of the world.' Discuss this statement in the light of John 1:1–14.
- Rev Stephen Dawes also wrote a translation of John 1:1–14 using 'idea' for 'word'. How does this further your understanding of this passage?

Prayer
O God, we thank You for all You give us,
    for life and health, for our families and friends,
    for the beauty of Your creation
    and all the kindness and love we receive.
    Most of all, we thank You for giving Your Son to be our Saviour
    and Friend.
    May we show our gratitude by living our lives to please You
    and by showing Your love to others. Amen.
based on the Anglican Alternative Service Book

Pray for others
Pray for those whose dark deeds blind them to Christ
    for the victims of evil actions
    for those who work with victims of evil actions
    for those who radiate love and light
    for those who bring love and light into your life.

Meditation

One day, God said, 'Let there be Love'
And a child was born whose name was Light.
'I am the Light of the world', he said.
'If you follow me you shall not walk in darkness.'
By the Light, humanity was liberated,
The blind received sight
And to the poor, Good News came.

Today we celebrate the Light, celebrate the hope,
In unity and in diversity,
Because of the Light, the Cross and the Heart,
For the shalom of the world
Together we build the future in hope.

Bishop Hae-Jong Kim, Pittsburgh, USA

20 DEC

No room

In all major towns and cities we seem to have come to accept a certain amount of homelessness. If we think in terms of statistics rather than individuals, then it is easier to bury the problem in our minds. The trouble is, these statistics *are* individuals with their own story – each is made in the image of God.

Bible reading
Matthew 25:31–40

Context
Storm clouds are gathering for Jesus – the end of His ministry is in sight. Matthew brings together the teaching he remembers about the end of the age, a time thought to be imminent. In these darker parables from Jesus a theme is clear for the disciples, and for us. We, as disciples of Jesus, have to be alert and prepared for whatever happens and we also have to realise the uncomfortable truth of judgment.

The unique point in this passage is that it is no longer God who is the Judge but Jesus Himself; this is a blatant departure from the Old Testament ideas. Jesus has come, and when He comes again it will be in full glory and majesty before all the world.

This would *not* have been a popular idea for the scribes, Pharisees, Sadducees and teachers of the Law.

Reflection

Dave was a pleasant young man. He was a stranger in the city and, through an unfortunate chain of events, found himself with no money and nowhere to stay.

Not wanting to be branded a scrounger, he went onto the seafront and found a glass-sided shelter where he huddled, waiting for Christmas morning.

A local church, out on their weekly soup-run, came across Dave and gave him much-needed soup and sandwiches. But they also listened to him, made a few phone calls, then delivered him to a hostel for homeless men where they knew he would be given warmth, a bed and breakfast the next day. Dave asked them why they were bothering with him. Their answer was simply that Jesus had been born into a world which had no room for Him, and they were just following the teaching Jesus gave, to find room for the lonely and rejected.

I was privileged to see the look of surprised joy on Dave's face – somebody cared for him.

Power point

Jesus said: 'Whenever you did one of these things for someone overlooked or ignored, that was me – you did it to me' (Matt. 25:40, *The Message*).

Things to consider or discuss

- 'This life is the performance, not the rehearsal' – but are we still pretending this is a rehearsal? How can we change?
- How does the discipline of Advent devotions help us to 'be prepared'?
- Inviting strangers into the home may not be sensible procedure

today, but in what other ways can you make a contribution to the needy?

- 'Eternal punishment' appears to be a contradiction of a loving God. What does this mean to you?
- How do you combat 'compassion fatigue' with all the deserving charities laying claim to your interest and your purse?

Prayer

Thank You, Lord, for all that means 'home' to me,
    for childhood memories, for neighbours and friends,
    for all the sentimental reasons why home is special,
    for the personal photographs and possessions which have been
    gathered over the years.
Lord, may my home be one of prayer
    and peace, of warmth and welcome for all. Amen.

Pray for others

Pray for church kitchens and soup runs
    Crisis volunteers
    night-shelters and other organisations for the homeless
    for those who work with the disadvantaged and homeless
    for families who have been made homeless
    for those who have run away from home
    for those who seek to re-unite separated families.

Meditation

    Thou didst leave thy throne and thy kingly crown
    When thou camest to earth for me:
    But in Bethlehem's home was there found no room
    For thy holy nativity:
    O come to my heart, Lord Jesus,
    There is room in my heart for thee.
                Emily E.S. Elliott, 1836–97

21 DEC

Welcoming Jesus into our hearts

Have you ever thought how much of our Christmas story is rooted in the received pictures from art down the ages? The pale Mary clothed in costly blue robes, the wooden, Western-style mangers and reverent animals? Artistic interpretations have nurtured awe and wonder over the centuries, but we also need to seek a true picture of Jesus. A picture which offers meaningful interpretation is Holman Hunt's *The Light of the World*. The door to the heart can only be opened from the inside, Jesus enters by invitation.

Bible reading
Revelation 3:14–22

Context
These letters to the seven churches are fascinating but I think I have a soft spot for the church in Laodicea. For its time, it was a thriving commercial city, a banking centre, famous for its cloth industry and with a medical school with specialists in opthalmics. It had every modern amenity – for 2,000 years ago – and it basked in wealthy self-satisfaction. There are obvious parallels with our own situation; have we become so sophisticated and self-sufficient that we rely upon our human ingenuity and success?

We think we have everything, but God knows we are woefully inadequate, blind to our need and deaf to the Christ who would come in and share with us.

Reflection
In her Advent reflection *Here & There*, Jill Baker describes the difference between calling at a house in Britain and calling on people on the Caribbean island of St Vincent. Jill was used to going to the door and knocking, whereas in St Vincent the usual practice was to stand at the gate and shout. The custom worked perfectly with the open doors and windows in that part of the world, but Jill mentioned the sadness that she was rarely invited inside lest she saw the flies and the chaos of everyday life. How different is the picture

John draws for us of Jesus standing at the door of our hearts. He offers to come right inside, to share in our cooking smells, to see all our inadequacies, to love us in the chaos, to be alongside us in every way. Are there areas of your life which you would prefer to keep hidden from Jesus?

Power point
Jesus is not far removed and unconcerned: He is Immanuel – God *with* us.

Things to consider or discuss
- Holman Hunt's conversion was mirrored in his picture *The Light of the World*. In what way would a picture portray your own meeting with Jesus?
- Discuss people whose conversions have inspired you.
- How do you feel the Lord's presence in the chaos of your day?
- Will you allow Jesus to transform those darker corners of your life with His light and joy?
- Have you spent Christmas in another country and if so, how did the customs vary?
- Where do you see the dangers of sentimentality masking the truth of the nativity?

Prayer
Lord, forgive me that I don't want to be caught unawares by You coming into my life, I want time to prepare and be ready for Your coming. The only thing is, I'm often so caught up in other things, time passes by, and I'm still not ready. Help me to accept that I may never be ready, but You are. Come to my heart with the peace of Your accepting love – come now in the quiet of this moment.

Pray for others
Pray for our brothers and sisters in other parts of the world
in the Carribean, South America
Asia, Africa
Australia, Europe
North America.

Meditation

Help me, Lord, to live this day in the light of your coming.
Give me the strength to face things I am putting off;
apologies
I need to utter, peace I need to make, kindness I need to show
And, above all, to be at peace with you that I may be ready
whenever You call. Amen.

Jill Baker

Suggestions for Group Work Week 3

Prayer

Use the prayer from 18 December.

Bible reading

John 1:1–14 with the context.

Discussion

- Say why you chose the Christmas card you have brought along and how you feel the card bears the message of Christ's birth.
- Each member choose a discussion topic from the week.

Prayer

Choose a prayer from the week to close.

---

1. This takes place at Wintershall, Bramley, near Guildford, Surrey, England.

WEEK 4
Joy to the World!

22 DEC

The birth of the Messiah will bring joy to the world

Zechariah the priest served in the Temple at Jerusalem and tradition has it that he and Elizabeth lived in the little village of Ein Karem just a short distance from the Holy City. So it was quite a journey for the young Mary to travel from Nazareth to visit her cousin and so understandably she made more than a weekend of it!

Bible reading
Luke 1:39–49

Context
The ancient mind set much store by supernatural birth of great figures. Let's look at the Old Testament for revered characters like Isaac and Samuel. Isaac's parents, Abraham and Sarah, thought they were 'too old' to have children and Sarah was quite certain that she was barren. For poor Hannah, we have the vivid picture of her desperate prayers for a son (1 Sam. 1:10–13) and for both women the Bible records that nothing is impossible with God.

Isaiah's famous prophecy: 'The virgin will be with child and will give birth to a son, and will call him Immanuel' (Isa. 7:14) was uttered in a time of crisis for the Jewish nation, some 600 years before the birth of Jesus. In the face of impending doom, this prophecy was a sign of hope and reassurance – God was still there.

Reflection

Isn't it wonderful to be able to share your news with someone who understands? What a close bond there must have been between Mary and the older Elizabeth. The story reads as if Elizabeth were the first person Mary wanted to be with. Elizabeth too was the recipient of God's loving mercy, she also was carrying a son. Both women were caught up in the miracle of pregnancy and both were humbly aware that their sons would belong to God. Excitement, yes, but also anxiety and trepidation – childbirth was fraught with danger in those times. But there is another facet of these two expectant mothers which shines down the generations – serene faith and obedience. An acceptance that even though they did not understand, they could trust in their God. If only we could be more like that.

Power point

The angel said to Mary: 'The holy one to be born will be called the Son of God' (Luke 1:35).

Things to consider or discuss

- Imagine what an awe-inspiring building the Temple must have been, especially when most people lived in tents, caves and small, flat-roofed houses.
- With the miracles of modern science, previously infertile women are enabled to give birth. How much should the desire of the mother be weighed against the needs of the unborn child?
- Consider the similarities between a present-day child's christening and the ancient presentation at the Temple.
- If you are a mother, reflect on your feelings just before the birth.
- Does the birth of a baby help your faith?

Prayer

Thank You, Lord, for the ones with whom I can share my news. The ones who will jump for joy with me and not be jealous – those who share my interests and faith.

Thank You for those heartbeat moments when I know my life is guided and blessed and that I am held in Your eternal love.

Pray for others

Pray for midwives, community nurses and health visitors
    for the staff of hospital paediatric units
    for the inventors of life-saving equipment for babies
    for families expecting a new arrival
    for those parents whose babies have died.

Meditation

    My cousin Mary came to me today.
    She is with child, yet she crossed the wild hill country just to be
      with me.
    There was joy, beyond all reason, at our meeting.
    And I take this for a sign that between her son and mine
    Will be a deep affinity, stronger than kinship's tie ...
    I may not live to see my child full-grown,
    But I will no longer speculate about the future,
    I will wait, like Mary, upon the Lord:
    Not in anxiety, but in peace – trusting His Word.
              Susan Brown [1]

23 DEC

Another journey

Yesterday we were thinking of Mary travelling from Nazareth to visit
her cousin Elizabeth. Today we see her next journey – to Bethlehem.
Almost the same route but taking a left turn away from Jerusalem to
David's city where Joseph had to register for the census. Yesterday,
it was an excited young girl rushing off to share her news – today,
it is an apprehensive first-time mother taking a precarious and
uncomfortable trek.

Bible reading

Luke 2:1–5

Context

'Seeing that the time has come for the house census, it is necessary to compel all those, who for any cause whatsoever are residing outside their districts to return to their own homes, that they may both carry out the regular order of the census. And may diligently attend to the cultivation of their allotments.'

This is a fragment of an actual government edict from Egypt at around the same time Caesar Augustus was checking on his taxpayers. Isn't it ironic that the census and the taxman are still part of our lifestyle! Our wonderful God uses the irritations and constraints of regulations to ensure His Son is born in Bethlehem, just as Micah had prophesied a few hundred years before (Micah 5:2).

Reflection

Had Luke been able to spend time with Mary in those volatile days when Paul was first arrested? When the nucleus of Jesus' followers were both irritant and attraction, was Mary sharing those things which she had kept in her heart for possibly over 40 years? Luke tells us at the very beginning of his Gospel that he had carefully investigated *everything* surrounding the Person of Jesus and, surely, such intimate details could only have come from one source. Look again at these brief verses – and imagine the picture behind them. Their journey was compulsory, the law was enforced by an occupying power, Joseph had to leave his business, childbirth was dangerous. What tensions! And, in a story where our principle thoughts are with Mary, let's pause to remember the man who loved her, who stood by her and protected her, Nazareth's carpenter, Joseph.

Power point

The angel of the Lord said: 'Joseph son of David, do not be afraid to take Mary home as your wife, because what is conceived in her is from the Holy Spirit. She will give birth to a son, and you are to give him the name Jesus, because he will save his people from their sins' (Matt. 1:20–21).

Things to consider and discuss

- Discuss the statement: 'Faith is putting your hand out in the darkness and finding it held.' When have you experienced this?
- Looking back on this past year, in what ways do you feel God has been guiding you?
- What has been an important moment of faith for you this year?
- What would Jeremiah 29:11 have meant to the devout Joseph?
- How does the beautiful carol 'Silent Night' equate with the realities of childbirth and a cattle stall in what was, for Mary, a strange town?

Prayer

Lord, I want to thank You for those who have guided and supported me. Parents, or others, who cuddled and changed me, fed me and dressed me, gave me my first words and held my hand for my first steps. I don't often think about those things, Lord, but I am deeply grateful. I pray in the name of Jesus my Lord. Amen.

Pray for others

Pray for all who are making journeys during this Advent season
    for those travelling known to us
    for all professional drivers, pilots and sea captains
    for those who work in the hotel industry at this busy time
    for people working in the growing tourist markets
    for those who work in government
    and in local government.

Meditation

    Light from a stained glass window –
    Peals from an ancient spire,
    A crib in a special corner, carols from the choir:
    The mysteries of whispered prayers quietly rise above
    To God, who sent a baby, to bless us with his love.

                Edwin Jukes

24 DEC

The joy of God's wonderful world

The photography from space helps us to grasp the stunning beauty of our world.

It also helps to put the vast distances into perspective, and place ourselves in the macro spec of history.

Bible reading
Genesis 1:1–10

Context
These opening verses of Genesis have been called the Overture for the whole Bible. Here we meet God in the very beginning of all beginnings, the God of awe and majesty, power and might. God's 'Word' brought order out of chaos, and His almighty power created the world as we understand it. The purpose of these verses was to put God at the centre of everything known and unknown, to acknowledge human frailty before the Creator and to see His glory in the wonders of nature. How truly amazing then to transfer this 'Word' to Jesus, to identify His deity as the Word made flesh. When we touch this area of mystery we find ourselves humbly having to leave calculations and proof behind and step out in faith and trust. This is the God we adore whose Son Jesus came to breathe life and joy into our lives.

Reflection
On Christmas Eve 1968, three men were orbiting the moon. These US astronauts were front-page news back then, but by now, their names have lost their immediate familiarity. However, I remember listening spellbound to the voices of Frank Borman, Jim Lovell and Bill Anders that night as they read out to the world below the first 10 verses of the book of Genesis. They closed their contact with Mission Control by saying: 'And from the crew of Apollo 8 we pause with good night, good luck, merry Christmas and God bless all of you on the good earth.' Millions watched their television screens as these

men made the first manned orbit of the moon – the same moon which had shone down on Bethlehem 2,000 years before.

Power point

'When I consider your heavens, the work of your fingers, the moon and the stars, which you have set in place, what is man that you are mindful of him …?' (Psa. 8:3)

Things to consider or discuss

- What message would you choose to send back from space?
- Which part of creation speaks to you of God's power and glory?
- Our God who created the universe, created you. How do you respond to that?
- The mystery of the Nativity is more than our human minds can understand. So how do you approach the awesome fact of God being born into his world?
- Is there anything you would rather God hadn't created?

Prayer

Lord of all life, below, above,
Your light is truth, Your warmth is love.
Centre and soul of every sphere
Yet to each loving heart – so near.
Lord, I want to place You at the centre of my life.

Oliver Wendell Holmes (adapted)

Pray for others

Pray for people working in the orbiting international space station
for astronomers who help us to marvel at the stars and galaxies
for public figures who are not embarrassed to mention their faith
for wild-life photographers on land, in the sea and in the air that
we may appreciate God's creation
for Bible translators and church leaders.

Meditation

O God, how full of wonder and splendour you are!
When I gaze into star-studded skies

And attempt to comprehend the vast distances,
I contemplate in utter amazement my Creator's concern for me.
I am dumbfounded that you should care personally about me.
O God, how full of wonder and splendour you are!

Psalm 8 (from *Psalms Now*, Leslie F. Brandt[2])

25 DEC

Christmas Day

At last! It is Christmas Day. In a strange way, the whole world seems
to have been driving towards this day; an inexplicable momentum
has propelled us through Advent. For some reason, this time of year
has a special atmosphere, people really want to be pleasant and
for good things to happen 'because it's Christmas'. Let's enjoy every
minute!

Bible reading
Luke 2:4–7

Context
So much is made of the innkeeper's words, 'No room' and yet when
we actually read the narrative in Luke's Gospel, no innkeeper gets
a mention! What we know is that Bethlehem was over capacity
because of the census and all the guest-rooms were occupied. For
Mary and Joseph, the only private area they could find for childbirth
away from strangers, was in the stable. Here, Mary could be attended
by a Bethlehem midwife and her cries muffled by cave walls.

I have not been present at a birth, but I was privileged to be there
minutes afterwards and witness a father take his first daughter in his
arms. The total wonder, relief and joy of the moment could only be
expressed by tears. It was a holy and unrepeatable moment. Mary
had given birth to her first child and I think we can be pretty sure
that as Joseph gathered Jesus in his arms for the first time, he felt the
same tears of wonder, relief and joy. This was his son and yet not
his son.

Reflection

Dr Billy Graham's crusades are almost legendary, with millions of people worldwide being brought to know the Lord through his preaching and challenge. This is what he wrote in December 1971 in *Decision* magazine about the Incarnation:

> The incarnation of Jesus Christ is not merely a doctrinal tenet about which theologians of different schools may hold differing views. It is a glorious reality, a wondrous fact apart from which there can be no salvation for sinful men. Who in the world that Rome rules at the time could possibly believe that this little baby in a stable was the great God of creation come in the flesh? This child nestled in Mary's arms would be both God and man united in one person, never again to be separated. This is the glorious mystery of the Incarnation ...

Power point

'Holy, holy, holy is the Lord God Almighty,
Who was, and is, and is to come.'
(Rev. 4:8)

Things to consider or discuss

- If you are a parent, recall how you felt on first holding your child.
- What is the hardest part of watching children grow up?
- Is there 'a child within you' and how do you express that?
- What part of Christmas Day do you most enjoy?
- How would you like to spend Christmas Day differently?
- Consider surprising someone with a visit or phone-call.

Prayer

Jesus, Prince of Peace ... grant me peace this day.
Jesus, born in Bethlehem ... be born in me this day.
Jesus, cradled and adored ... hold me in Your love this day.
Jesus, yesterday, today and forever ... guide my life this day and
always. Amen.

Pray for others

Lord, I pray for peace on earth and goodwill between all people.

Meditation

We are talking about the birth of a child,
Not the revolutionary act of a strong man,
Not the breathtaking discovery of a sage,
Not the pious act of a saint.
It really passes all understanding: the birth of a child
Is to bring the great turning round of all things,
Is to bring salvation and redemption to the whole human race.
What kings and statesmen, philosophers and artists,
Founders of religions and moral teachers vainly strive for,
Now comes about through a newborn child.

Dietrich Bonhoeffer[3]

26 DEC

Joy is touched by pain

Christmas is not a happy period for everyone. In fact, many more people than we realise dread this time of year. And then there are those millions of our brothers and sisters whose circumstances preclude any joy ... the victims of war, civil war, famine, disease ... for them life is brutal.

Bible reading
Matthew 2:13–23

Context
Here we face the miserable combination of absolute power and raging jealousy – evils we find in many areas of life today. This is a section of the gospel we prefer to avoid, for it breaks in on the joy of Christ's birth with unacceptable murder. With all the decorations around and the presents given and received, we do not want our festive aura to be broken. But life is full of contrast: joy and tears, light and dark, good and evil, life and death – we cannot escape.

Herod's deluded orders were to destroy any possibility that his own power might be weakened by this child born to be King. His jealousy brought heartache to the mothers in Bethlehem but he could not eradicate God's Messiah. For Mary and Joseph it meant yet another journey, this time, most likely by night, clutching the infant Lord, escaping to the safety of Egypt.

Reflection
On Boxing Day 2004 the world learned a word previously only understood by a few – Tsunami. Probably more than 250,000 people lost their lives in the disaster which hit many countries in Asia following the earthquake. Millions more were made homeless. The statistics were beyond belief and the cruel human tragedy stunned the world. Many cried, 'Where is God in this?' but never before have the people of all nations made such a spontaneous and generous outpouring of cash for medicine, shelter and food.

The destruction and hopelessness, the pain, bereavement and shock of this terrible event, has made yet another mark in history, another entry in the catalogue of human misery where the innocent always suffer.

Does this memory move you to be more grateful for your own situation and to appreciate anew the gift of life?

Power point
'... the LORD was not in the earthquake' (1 Kings 19:11).

Things to consider or discuss
- When tragedy strikes how do we find God's love?
- Reflect quietly on how pain has helped your reliance on God, and the times when God seemed very far away.
- How can we bring comfort to those nearest to us who are going through painful periods in marriage, or with children or parents?
- Consider the number of times the television has shown fleeing refugees and pose the question – are we numb to such pictures?
- Why do we feel better when we have made a practical contribution to a disaster fund or favourite charity?

Prayer

Lord, when my confidence is shaken, when my world collapses,
help me to trust. When I don't understand help me to hang on to
my faith, if only by my fingertips. In these moments, may I feel the
warm encircling of Your Holy Spirit. Immanuel … God is with us.
Thanks be to God.

Pray for others

Pray for all those involved in rebuilding from the Tsunami disaster
    for those who lost loved ones who were never found
    for the orphans of the disaster
    for those who will be killed on the roads this week
    for closer international understanding and co-operation.
Give thanks for the spirit of human kindness.

Meditation

When innocence is fractured by nature's shifting force;
And paradise is ruptured and life is swept off course –
We come to pray our questions.
We come to share our grief in this, our act of worship,
To say that we believe.

How dare we speak of heaven
Made human for our sakes,
Or preach a loving Father
When seas and mountains quake?
We dare because our story speaks of a love
That came to bear the cost of dying
And still would do the same.

Gareth Hill (GraceNotes Music, 2005)

27 DEC

The shepherds' joy

The shepherds cared for their sheep; they were protectors, vets, midwives, providers of food and water – 24/7. In His teaching, Jesus would use the shepherd image with powerful effect. Jesus called Himself 'the good shepherd'.

Bible reading
Luke 2:8–20

Context
For some reason shepherds were despised people, but they were also the couriers of ancient times. Wandering from place to place for pasture, they carried the news – and the gossip – these were the 'broadcasters' that God used. How extraordinary that these rough men of the hills were the people God chose to be the first evangelists!

Luke's birth narrative seems full of angels – Gabriel appeared to Zechariah and to Mary, and then a 'whole company' of them burst into praise for the shepherds. The translation of the Greek word for 'angel' means messenger or agent, and these messengers had appeared in the past to Abraham, Gideon, Elijah and David, to name just a few. The message was always an assurance of God's presence.

Reflection
Sitting in a cave in the area of the Shepherds' Fields outside Bethlehem, I looked at the candle-blackened roof. I could imagine the shepherds wearily propped against the stone walls with the chief shepherd stretched across the doorway to keep the sheep inside. All safe and quiet for the night. A night that changed their lives! Into these very fields, around these stones and pathways, the Lord God shone His glory.

Have you ever thought about what happened to these men and boys? They were the first people to speak about the Messiah, the Saviour that they had all longed for – they had *seen Him*! They certainly 'spread the word' – could we call them the first 'Christians'?

Power point
Paul wrote: 'God chose the foolish things of the world to shame the wise; God chose the weak things of the world to shame the strong' (1 Cor. 1:27).

Things to consider or discuss
- Reflect on the paradox: shepherds were held in contempt yet Jesus called Himself the good shepherd.
- Where do we see 'the glory of the Lord' today?
- Who do you rely upon to know what is best?
- Think about the times when you found God in unexpected places and people.
- The shepherds left what they knew to go where God had told them – has there been an occasion when you stepped out in faith?
- Pause to consider that *we* are Christ's messengers today. What does that mean in your life?

Prayer
Lord, open my eyes to see Your glory
in the eyes of a child, in the petal of a flower,
in the sound of the waves, in the song of a bird,
in the shafts of light through the clouds,
in the thrill of music.
Glory to God in the highest and on earth, peace for all people.
Amen.

Pray for others
Pray for all farmers
and shepherds
for all who work in agriculture and horticulture
for veterinary surgeons
for animal welfare organisations.
Thank God for the 'angels' you have met.

Meditation

I stood one night by a stable door,
It was cold and the stars shone bright;
I could just see a newborn babe
Bathed in mysterious light,
But I didn't know then, this was the Christ-child;
I didn't know then, this was my King.

Shepherds left their sheep on the hill,
Their faces filled with joy –
They sang and danced and prayed and laughed,
This was no ordinary boy:
Then my heart opened, I saw the Christ-child,
I cried: 'Messiah, this is my King'.

28 DEC

Wise men overjoyed

Whoever these mysterious figures were, they had travelled a long
way. If they were rich enough to travel with such gifts, they were
equally rich enough to be worth robbing, so their journey was not
without danger. Therefore, it is highly likely that they travelled with
a large entourage of servants. When we look at them in this light, we
see how this story was important for Matthew to tell.

Bible reading
Matthew 2:1–12

Context
The Jewish Scripture is made up of The Law, the Prophets and
The Writings and within The Writings we find Wisdom Literature:
Proverbs, Job and Ecclesiastes. This underlines how highly prized
Wisdom was in the Middle East. This is what it says in the 28th
chapter of Job: '... where can wisdom be found? ... God understands

the way to it and he alone knows where it dwells …' (vv.12,23). We even find Paul equating Jesus as the wisdom and power of God (1 Cor. 1:18–25).

So the Magi (the 'three kings') risked their lives to find the new King. It is only the carol that calls these visitors 'kings'; Matthew called them 'Magi' meaning 'wise men'. These 'wise men' – and possibly wise women too – risked their lives to worship a child they believed was born to be a great King. Somewhere in Bethlehem, between the time of the census and Joseph and Mary's escape into Egypt, the foreign visitors bowed to a mightier wisdom and power.

Reflection

Last year I was surprised how many Christmas cards depicted the 'three kings', in various artistic representations. I suppose the aspect of their gifts make them popular Christmas images. Let's think of those symbolic gifts for a moment: gold for a King, frankincense for a priest, and myrrh, a versatile spice, for both joyous occasions and also for embalming the dead. How perfectly these gifts matched the life and mission of the Lord Jesus. Among all the billions of people who have been born, only Jesus was born for God's specific reason to bring light and salvation to human hearts. As the traditional carol says: 'Christ was born to save.' Jesus, our King, our mediator and Saviour, was born *for us*.

Power point

'Nicodemus brought a mixture of myrrh and aloes … Taking Jesus' body, the two of them wrapped it, with the spices, in strips of linen. This was in accordance with Jewish burial customs' (John 19:39–40).

Things to consider or discuss

- Image you were a Bethlehem innkeeper, how would you react to all the foreigners?
- If the gifts of gold, frankincense and myrrh were appropriate symbolic gifts for Jesus in those times, what gifts would you consider suitable for our Saviour today?
- What do you think the wise men thought when they reached where Jesus was?
- What characteristics do you admire in the Magi?

- Compare the Magi entering His 'home', seeing the baby Jesus and believing in Him, with the disciple John going inside the empty tomb and believing (John 20:8).
- What gifts would you like to offer to the newborn King?

Prayer

Jesus, born to be Messiah, guide us by your star,
Guide us as we follow, not certain where it leads,
But we are your pilgrim people,
We will follow.
We make our prayer through him, who became one of us
that we may become one with him – Jesus Christ our Lord. Amen.

Liz Law

Pray for others

Pray for people who feel that they are 'foreigners' in the land where they live

for the millions of refugees
for world leaders seeking to follow paths of peace
for those who work for reconciliation
for Amnesty International and The United Nations
for a just and equal sharing of resources and knowledge
for others to know the priceless gift of the Holy Spirit in
their lives.

What have you not done this Christmas that you meant to do?
Where has God surprised you with joy?

Meditation

Say, shall we give him, in costly devotion
Odours of Edom and offerings divine,
Gems from the mountain and pearls of the ocean,
Myrrh from the forest or gold from the mine?

Vainly we offer each ample oblation;
Vainly with gifts would his favour secure;

Richer by far is the heart's adoration;
Dearer to God are the prayers of the poor.

Reginald Heber, 1783–1826

Suggestions for Group Work Week 4

Bible reading

Luke 1:26–38 and Luke 2:1–7

Reflection

Using a large map of the world, map pins and strips of narrow ribbon, begin by attaching a ribbon with a pin to your country and also a pin and ribbon to the Holy Land. Then ask members of the group to place their pin in a country where they have family or friends. The ribbon should be long enough to reach from the map to the seated person, or you may wish to wind the ribbons loosely round the base of a central cross.

When all the ribbons and pins are in place, light a candle at the foot of the cross as you bring these various countries to the Lord in silent prayer. Reflect on how many countries are linked by your one group.

Discussion

Choose discussion questions from separate days in the week.

Prayer

A responsive prayer: 'Bethlehem Intercessions'
Written by Rev Liz Law in Bethlehem 2004

L: Jesus, born as Saviour for all mankind,
As we lift our hearts to you in prayer,
Come down to meet us here:
Jesus born as one of us
R: *Hear our prayer*

L: Jesus, Immanuel,
We give you thanks and praise;

May we rejoice with shepherds and angels.
Speak to our hearts and minds again
Refresh us and renew us, your pilgrim people:
Jesus, born as one of us

R: *Hear our prayer*

L: Jesus, born of David's line,
We hold before you those who lead,
In our Churches and in our country –
We pray with longing hearts for truth and justice.
Speak to this hungry generation of your heavenly kingdom.
Jesus, born as one of us

R: *Hear our prayer*

L: Jesus, born into an occupied land
Who found no room at the Inn,
We pray today for those living under oppression.
Your image lives in each one –
Bring down the walls which separate us –
Make strong in our hearts what unites us –
help us to build bridges across all that divides us.
Jesus, born as one of us

R: *Hear our prayer*

To end, the Leader places some small, wrapped gifts in a basket, each person takes one, then 'gives' it to another member of the group.

Close with the blessing from Romans 15:13:
'May the God of hope fill you with all joy and peace as you trust in him, so that you may overflow with hope by the power of the Holy Spirit.'

---

1. Susan Brown, *Liturgy of Life* (NCEC, 1991) p.98.

2. Leslie F. Brandt, *Psalms Now* (Concordia Publishing House, 1996).

3. Dietrich Bonhoeffer, from *The Mystery of Holy Night* (Crossroad, 1996).

WEEK FIVE
Into the New Year

29 DEC

The joy of God's presence

Throughout the Old Testament we find the contrast between the
revelations of God's nature. On the one hand there is the God
of wrath and judgment, and on the other there is the tender,
compassionate side of God. Whichever aspect of God the Israelites
were experiencing, the truth remained – He was always there.

Bible reading
Zephaniah 3:9–17

Context
The prophet Zephaniah is one of the lesser-known men of the
Old Testament but, as far as worldly status goes, he was the most
influential – the great-great-grandson of King Hezekiah. As such
he would have moved in grand circles with the rich, powerful and
educated minds of the day. He would have held a keen grasp on the
political situation facing the Israelites and, like all other prophets, he
equated disaster with the consequence of turning away from God.
Zephaniah uttered his prophecies just before the great reforms of
King Josiah, so maybe at least a few people were listening to him!

For Zephaniah, the Day of the Lord would bring judgment
and retribution but also ultimately there would be great rejoicing
and peace.

Reflection

'The LORD your God is with you ...' cries Zephaniah across the centuries – and here we are, having just celebrated the birth of Immanuel: God with us! The royal-blooded prophet could see the nations bringing ruin upon themselves because of their behaviour, even his own nation.

When we look out over our world, it sometimes feels like little has changed – social wrongs, superstitions, treachery and self-satisfaction. We see the consequences of violating the earth's resources and maintaining the unjust balance of trade. How can we not speak up for justice and peace, how can we not rejoice when, by the power of the Holy Spirit, God is with us in the human face of Jesus.

Power point

'Be glad and rejoice with all your heart ...' (Zeph. 3:14).

Things to consider or discuss

- What makes your heart rejoice today?
- How do the consequences of how we live affect other people?
- In what ways can ordinary people make a difference to global problems?
- Think how you felt when God seemed far away.
- When do you feel God, or Jesus, is with you?
- Consider how God has blessed you this Christmas.

Prayer

I know that my Redeemer lives –
what joy the blest assurance gives!

Thank You, Lord, that wherever I am, I am always in the same place ... held in the hollow of Your hand. You love me, forgive me and accept me just as I am – You never give up on me – You never leave me. Thank You, my Lord and my King.

Pray for others

Pray for those who have been involved in fund-raising over this Christmas period

for community volunteers

for those who volunteer to work overseas
for people who make us laugh.
Give thanks for the ones who have given us happiness
for all who openly share their Christian faith.

Meditation

Take time to laugh, it is the music of the soul;
Take time to play, it is the source of perpetual youth.
Take time to pray, it is the greatest power on earth;
Take time to be friendly, it is the road to happiness ...

Anonymous

30 DEC

Joy to the faithful

Eugene Peterson's version of the Bible, *The Message*, describes
Simeon as a man who 'lived in prayerful expectancy'. I think that's
a lovely phrase. Both Simeon and Anna had dedicated their lives to
God and waited in sure and certain hope of great things.

Bible reading
Luke 2:25–38

Context
Joseph and Mary bring Jesus to the Temple in accordance with
Scripture (Exod. 12:1–2; Lev. 12). But there is more to this account
than two elderly people rejoicing in the young child. Simeon's great
thanksgiving to God breaks out of the Temple culture, tearing down
in a most astonishing way the divisions between Jew and Gentile
– the Messiah will be for *all* people.

Luke's Gospel is sometimes called the 'social Gospel' and in
Simeon's prayer, known as the Nunc Dimitis, he points away
from religious exclusiveness to the universality of Jesus' mission;
something Paul will underline in his letter to the Colossian Christians:
'Here there is no Greek or Jew, circumcised or uncircumcised ...
slave or free, but Christ is all, and is in all' (Col. 3:11).

Reflection

Do you ever feel life is geared to the under thirties? And to be an over-forty-something is oblivion? Let us, those of us who are older, take heart – in faith age has no ceiling, only a need for enthusiasm, hope and commitment.

Dear old Anna and Simeon had experienced many shattered dreams in their long lives – who hasn't? But they were not disillusioned, they had not given up. Nor were they gently dozing in a corner! No, they were alert and welcoming to all visitors to the Temple, and especially the children. Their cameo appearance in Luke's story, when Jesus was eight days old, gives us much to think about regarding our attitudes to age.

Power point

'Wait for the LORD and keep his way' (Psa. 37:34).

Things to consider or discuss

- It has been said: salvation is offered to all, but it has to be considered by each. How do you understand this statement?
- Anna was a great woman of prayer. In what ways would you like to deepen your prayer life?
- How do we show our respect for the experience of men and women where age has made them frail?
- Imagine you met Simeon after Mary and Joseph had left the Temple. What would you ask him?
- How difficult is it to keep 'prayerfully expectant'?
- What 'swords' pierce the heart of every mother?

Prayer

Lord, I pray for the quiet perseverance and faith shown in Simeon and Anna. Help me to guard against discouragement, and fix my eyes on Jesus. Thank You for the joy that each child brings and may this day be filled with faith, hope and love.

Pray for others

Pray for any elderly people in your family
    for all who are housebound through frailty
    for experienced leaders and teachers

for those who work with caring for the elderly in the community
for those who live in residential homes
for old people whose young outlook and hope inspires us
for the aged who feel forgotten and unloved.

Meditation

Paul wrote to the first Christians in Rome:
Love from the centre of who you are ...
Don't burn out – be cheerfully expectant.
Don't quit in hard times; pray all the harder.
Help needy Christians,
Be inventive in hospitality.
Rom. 12:9–12, *The Message*

31 DEC

Stepping into the new year with joy

The last few hours of the year. Looking back can evoke happy
memories or make us gasp at how fast the months have gone. The
media wallows in the nostalgia of past events; what kind of a year
has it been for you?

Bible reading

Matthew 5:1–16

Context

One of my favourite places is the Mount of Beatitudes overlooking
the Sea of Galilee. Sitting in the grounds of the Church
commemorating the Beatitudes, feeling the warmth of the sun and
listening to the bird-song, I can almost hear Jesus teaching these
'Attitudes for Life', a teaching so contrary to our human instincts yet
the very basis of our discipleship. Here was His manifesto, this was
the way He lived and these are the attributes every Christian has to
take on board. We shall be blessed when we can turn the material
world around and find God before self, profit, possessions, power
and might.

Our lives have to mirror these Beatitudes before we begin to witness to the presence of the living Lord Jesus in our lives.

Reflection

One of the most influential spiritual writers, Henri Nouwen, gave an inspired insight into the Beatitudes: 'These words offer us a self-portrait of Jesus ... the whole message of the gospel is this: "Become like Jesus." Become like Jesus! What a challenge!'

Over these weeks of Advent, building to the celebration of our Lord's birth, we have traced prophecy about the Messiah, read of the birth in Bethlehem, and reflected on the impact of Jesus of Nazareth on people's lives. Now, as we come to the end of our Advent study we can turn to face our new year with a motivation to act upon some of the things we have shared. Jesus *lived out* the Beatitudes and He calls us to engage in this Christian lifestyle, not just for the coming year, but for life.

Power point

Jesus promised: 'I am with you always, to the very end of the age' (Matt. 28:20).

Things to consider and discuss

- What are your New Year resolutions?
- What are your spiritual New Year resolutions?
- Donald Soper, later Lord Soper, called the Christian life 'the Christian Adventure' – how would you describe the Christian life today?
- Discuss the idea that each year we are a little older and a little wiser!
- Consider meeting with someone, or maybe with two others to form a prayer link for the coming year.

Prayer

Eternal God, as we come to the end of another year, we thank You that throughout it all You have been with us. We ask forgiveness for anything hurtful and wrong we have done. Help us now to make a new beginning with the love, peace and joy of Jesus Christ in our hearts today and for the coming year. Amen.

Pray for others

At the beginning of a New Year:
Pray for world peace
    peace between communities
    peace between neighbours
    peace between families
    peace between churches
    peace in the hearts of those we have prayed for during Advent
    peace in the hearts of those we love.

Take a look at your prayer journal – has God opened a new way for you?

Meditation

Another year is dawning,
Dear God, in all I do, in working or in resting,
I'll live this year in you.
Another year of progress,
Another year for praise, another year of knowing
Your presence in all my days.
Another year of blessing,
Another year to prove in every sphere of living
The wonders of your love.

Based on Frances Ridley Havergal, 1836–1879

List people to pray for this year

Write a prayer asking for God's help in keeping a Spiritual
New Year Resolution or some personal need.

National Distributors

UK: (and countries not listed below)
CWR, Waverley Abbey House, Waverley Lane, Farnham, Surrey GU9 8EP.
Tel: (01252) 784700 Outside UK +44 1252 784700

AUSTRALIA: CMC Australasia, PO Box 519, Belmont, Victoria 3216. Tel: (03) 5241 3288

CANADA: Cook Communications Ministries, PO Box 98, 55 Woodslee Avenue, Paris, Ontario.
Tel: 1800 263 2664

GHANA: Challenge Enterprises of Ghana, PO Box 5723, Accra. Tel: (021) 222437/223249 Fax: (021) 226227

HONG KONG: Cross Communications Ltd, 1/F, 562A Nathan Road, Kowloon. Tel: 2780 1188 Fax: 2770 6229

INDIA: Crystal Communications, 10-3-18/4/1, East Marredpalli, Secunderabad – 500026, Andhra Pradesh.
Tel/Fax: (040) 27737145

KENYA: Keswick Books and Gifts Ltd, PO Box 10242, Nairobi. Tel: (02) 331692/226047 Fax: (02) 728557

MALAYSIA: Salvation Book Centre (M) Sdn Bhd, 23 Jalan SS 2/64, 47300 Petaling Jaya, Selangor.
Tel: (03) 78766411/78766797 Fax: (03) 78757066/78756360

NEW ZEALAND: CMC Australasia, PO Box 36015, Lower Hutt. Tel: 0800 449 408 Fax: 0800 449 049

NIGERIA: FBFM, Helen Baugh House, 96 St Finbarr's College Road, Akoka, Lagos.
Tel: (01) 7747429/4700218/825775/827264

PHILIPPINES: OMF Literature Inc, 776 Boni Avenue, Mandaluyong City. Tel: (02) 531 2183 Fax: (02) 531 1960

SINGAPORE: Armour Publishing Pte Ltd, Block 203A Henderson Road, 11–06 Henderson Industrial Park,
Singapore 159546. Tel: 6 276 9976 Fax: 6 276 7564

SOUTH AFRICA: Struik Christian Books, 80 MacKenzie Street, PO Box 1144, Cape Town 8000.
Tel: (021) 462 4360 Fax: (021) 461 3612

SRI LANKA: Christombu Books, 27 Hospital Street, Colombo 1. Tel: (01) 433142/328909

TANZANIA: CLC Christian Book Centre, PO Box 1384, Mkwepu Street, Dar es Salaam. Tel/Fax: (022) 2119439

USA: Cook Communications Ministries, PO Box 98, 55 Woodslee Avenue, Paris, Ontario, Canada.
Tel: 1800 263 2664

ZIMBABWE: Word of Life Books, Shop 4, Memorial Building, 35 S Machel Avenue, Harare.
Tel: (04) 781305 Fax: (04) 774739

For email addresses, visit the CWR website: www.cwr.org.uk

CWR is a registered charity – number 294387

Day and Residential Courses
Counselling Training
Leadership Development
Biblical Study Courses
Regional Seminars
Ministry to Women
Daily Devotionals
Books and Videos
Conference Centre

Trusted all Over the World

CWR HAS GAINED A WORLDWIDE reputation as a centre of excellence for Bible-based training and resources. From our headquarters at Waverley Abbey House, Farnham, England, we have been serving God's people for 40 years with a vision to help apply God's Word to everyday life and relationships. The daily devotional *Every Day with Jesus* is read by nearly a million readers an issue in more than 150 countries, and our unique courses in biblical studies and pastoral care are respected all over the world. Waverley Abbey House provides a conference centre in a tranquil setting.

For free brochures on our seminars and courses, conference facilities, or a catalogue of CWR resources, please contact us at the following address.
CWR, Waverley Abbey House, Waverley Lane, Farnham, Surrey GU9 8EP, UK

Telephone: **+44 (0)1252 784700**
Email: **mail@cwr.org.uk**
Website: **www.cwr.org.uk**

CRUSADE FOR WORLD REVIVAL
Applying God's Word to everyday life and relationships

Cover to Cover Every Day

The latest daily reading notes from CWR, *Cover to Cover Every Day*.

- Short in-depth Bible study every day
- Full colour flap with maps, charts, photos or illustrations relevant to the study material
- Well-known contributors including R.T. Kendall, Jeff Lucas, Joel Edwards, Philip Greenslade ...
- Rolling five-year curriculum will cover every book of the Bible

Available bimonthly

£1.99 (plus p&p)

1744-0114

Annual UK subscription (six issues)

£11.50

(including p&p)

Cover to Cover

Cover to Cover takes you on a chronological journey through the Bible, following events as they actually happened. Featuring: a page-per-day reading plan, a 'bird's eye view' of each Bible book, charts, maps, illustrations, diagrams and comments from Selwyn Hughes and Trevor Partridge which will assist you in drawing a personal challenge or encouragement from each day's reading.

£9.95 (plus p&p)
ISBN: 1-85345-136-3

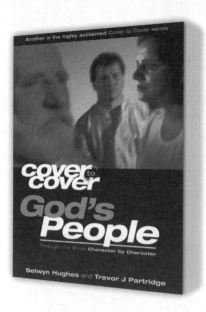

Cover to Cover God's People

Cover to Cover – God's People traces the amazing relationship between God and man. This one-year plan, which follows the phenomenal success of the original *Cover to Cover* title, profiles 58 of the Bible's most fascinating and instructive personalities. Selected verses from the Old and New Testaments reveal how God takes ordinary people and makes them extraordinary to fulfil His purpose.

£9.95 (plus p&p)
ISBN: 1-85345-160-6

Cover to Cover God's Story

Cover to Cover – God's Story is an exciting Bible-reading programme that takes you on a journey of discovery through Scripture. At the heart of this programme are the major covenants by which God expresses His love, and over the year you will be moved as you recognise how familiar stories and individual promises fit into the larger, coherent story of the Bible. *Cover to Cover – God's Story* is available as a beautifully designed colour softback book.

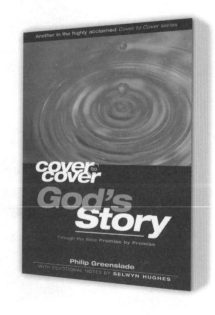

£9.95 (plus p&p)
ISBN: 1-85345-186-X

Prices correct at time of printing